The Politics of Chicano Liberation

The Politics of Chicano Liberation

Olga Rodríguez
Editor

PATHFINDER PRESS   NEW YORK

"The Struggle for Chicano Liberation" is
reprinted by permission of the *International
Socialist Review*. Copyright © 1971 by
International Socialist Review

Library of Congress Catalog Card Number 77-81292
ISBN cloth 0-87348-513-0 / paper 0-87348-514-9
Manufactured in the United States of America

Pathfinder Press
410 West Street, New York, NY 10014

Contents

Introduction

The year 1977 has seen broadside attacks on Chicano rights in every area of social, political, and economic life, as well as the beginning of motion of the Chicano community in response to these attacks.

On May 31, 1977, the U.S. Supreme Court ruled that, despite the proof of past discrimination, seniority systems that preserve and perpetuate job inequality are not necessarily illegal. This decision strikes a major blow to the decades-long battle by Chicanos, other oppressed national minorities, and women against discriminatory hiring and firing policies.

This ruling came on the heels of the decision by the California Supreme Court in the case of *Allan Bakke* v. *Board of Regents,* which abolishes special admissions programs for Chicano and other minority students in the California university system. Both the *Bakke* decision and the high court ruling on seniority lay the basis for a full-scale assault on the principle of affirmative action, and ultimately aim to wipe out the gains Chicanos and others have won in securing the better jobs, training, and education that have been closed to them for so long.

The attacks on equal education go further, as racist forces, with the support of Democratic and Republican politicians, move to dismantle bilingual-bicultural education programs. The racists are also mobilizing to end busing programs designed to enforce the rights of Chicanos and other minorities to attend the schools of their choice, including the better-equipped and better-staffed schools in predominantly Anglo communities.

Chicanas, who already must bear a major burden of the attacks on the Chicano community, face additional problems as women. Among these are attempts by the present Congress to cut off Medicaid funding for abortion—which will deny Chicanas access to safe, legal abortions—and the widespread sterilization abuse which particularly victimizes Chicanas.

A central axis of the capitalist offensive is the campaign against Mexicano, other Central and South American, and Caribbean immigrants without visas. The Carter administration's much-touted immigration policy is a blueprint for further victimizations and deportations of these immigrants, which also affect Chicanos.

The Chicano community and the working class as a whole are being forced to respond to these and other attacks by the capitalists, whose aim is to reverse the gains, drive down the wages, and curtail the democratic rights we have secured over the last several decades.

The most significant development in the fight against the capitalist offensive is the rise of a movement for democracy within one of the most powerful industrial unions in the United States. The challenge of Steelworkers Fight Back to the entrenched bureaucracy of the United Steelworkers of America offers Chicanos a glimpse of the kind of mighty allies that must and can be won to their struggle for equality, human dignity, and justice. The program of Fight Back in the February 1977 elections for international president of the steelworkers' union included the concept that rank-and-file workers have the right to democratically decide and advance their own interests above those of the bosses. But Fight Back did not stop there. Ed Sadlowski and the other Fight Back candidates raised the idea that the trade unions must join with Chicanos, Blacks, other oppressed national minorities, and women in their struggles for social and economic equality.

Chicanos are not only the allies of labor, but they are also an important component of it. As one of the most oppressed and exploited sections of the working class, Chicanos can be expected to be in the forefront of any development in the direction of transforming the unions into instruments of class struggle and class independence. The fact that Chicano steelworkers from Los Angeles to Detroit and from Pueblo to Chicago participated in the Fight Back campaign captures both the dual character of Chicano oppression and the dual sides of the struggle against it.

Steelworkers Fight Back not only ran a Chicano, Ignacio "Nash" Rodríguez, for international secretary, but also spoke out on issues of burning concern in the Chicano community. It took a position for the rights of undocumented workers, asserting that American workers have more in common with their Mexican and other brothers and sisters forced to search for jobs in the United States, than they have with their bosses and the government that seeks to deport these workers. This position is a radical departure from the long-standing chauvinist position of the present steel union officialdom and the rest of the AFL-CIO bureaucracy, who are among the most vociferous proponents of deportations.

The developing Fight Back movement in steel and the participation of Chicano workers in it from the beginning mark a new and important stage in the fight for Chicano liberation and the radicalization of the working class as a whole.

These developments bring into sharp relief the question of what strategy and program are needed to counter the attacks on Chicano rights.

The collection of articles in this book is offered as a contribution to the discussion on this question among Chicano activists. Together with the documents and reports in *Prospects for Socialism in America* (New York: Pathfinder Press, 1976), these materials outline the Socialist Workers Party's program for Chicano liberation. Two of the contributions printed here are programmatic documents adopted by the SWP at national conventions in 1971 and 1976. Also included in this collection are reports on the Chicano struggle to the national conventions that discussed and adopted the two documents. "The Struggle for Chicano Liberation" first appeared in the November 1971 *International Socialist Review,* and was printed as a pamphlet by Pathfinder Press in 1972. All the other articles appear publicly for the first time here.

This book reflects the continuity of the SWP's position on the national question in the United States as it applies to the Chicano people. While the SWP adopted its first programmatic document on the Chicano struggle in 1971, the participation of revolutionary socialists in the struggles goes back to the organizing efforts of *campesinos* in the 1930s and 1940s and before. The resolutions and reports contained in the following pages develop the SWP's positions on the rights of oppressed nationalities and national minorities to self-determination, positions which derive from the pioneering work of the Russian

Bolsheviks—particularly Lenin and Trotsky—on the national question.

This question has been thrust to the fore not just in the United States but in all the advanced capitalist countries, in the struggle for the conquest of power by the toiling masses.

The first section contains three articles that attempt to come to grips with the developments that led to the resurgence of Chicano nationalist consciousness in the 1960s. The first article, "The Forging of an Oppressed Nationality," by Antonio Camejo, traces some of the central events that helped to forge the native Mexican inhabitants of what is now the southwestern portion of the United States into a nationality distinct from any other in this country. Camejo takes these developments up to the struggles of the 1940s and 1950s, the period which helped to sow the seeds of Chicano nationalist consciousness that flowered in the 1960s.

"The Struggle for Chicano Liberation" and Antonio Camejo's report on it to the Twenty-fourth National Convention of the Socialist Workers Party in 1971, analyze and help explain the roots of Chicano nationalism, and set forth the revolutionary socialist analysis of the Chicano struggle and its dynamic as it emerged in the 1960s. It elaborates some of the key elements of a program that speaks to the needs of Chicanos, and advances the present struggles of the Chicano community toward the goal of full liberation.

The second part of this book, which includes "The Crisis of American Capitalism and the Struggle for Chicano Liberation" and the report on that document by myself to the Twenty-eighth National SWP Convention in 1976, complement the SWP's analysis of the new political situation arising from the changes in the world economic situation. This section takes into account the last five years of experience of the Chicano struggle, and as such is an indispensable tool for understanding and participating in the new struggles unfolding in the Chicano community.

The resurgence of Chicano nationalism occurred during the high point of the radicalization of the 1960s and early 1970s. The battles of the *campesinos* to unionize California's fields; the student and parent struggle for bilingual and bicultural education, Chicano studies programs, and open admissions in the universities; the rise of Chicana feminism; and the development of the Raza Unida parties—all took place during a period when the country's rulers had more leeway to make some concessions to the demands of the oppressed.

But the struggles of Chicanos today take place in a very different context, posing more fundamental questions of strategy. The framework now is one of deepening social and economic crises in the United States and on a world scale—a period when the capitalist rulers have less room for maneuver and are thus less able to grant the kinds of concessions necessary to meet the demands of the Chicano community. The Chicano movement is now obliged to defend even the meager gains of the 1960s and early 1970s which are under severe attack. The ruling class offensive is generating new struggles among Chicanos, which are part of the response by the working class as a whole as it begins to radicalize under the blows of the crisis. Despite temporary upturns in the economy, the future for Chicanos under capitalism is clearly one of increasing instability and insecurity, as we continue to be among those hit first and hardest.

The current government-led offensive to roll back the living standards and rights Chicanos won over the past decade illustrate the depth of Chicano oppression and indicate that the fight for Chicano liberation cannot be won short of a socialist revolution. These attacks are not only part of the capitalists' drive against working people as a whole, but they are also essential to the rulers' strategy of deepening existing divisions within the working class by forcing one of its most vulnerable sections to bear a major share of the burden of the economic crisis.

To try to prevent us from searching for collective solutions to the problems that confront us all, the capitalists utilize the racism they have so carefully nurtured within the working class against Chicanos and other oppressed national minorities. Together with sexism, racism is one of the most powerful weapons they have to undercut the elementary class solidarity and consciousness necessary to effectively counter the ruling class offensive. Evidence of the initial success of this divide and rule strategy is everywhere, as the rulers drive full speed ahead with their austerity program; cutbacks in social services; high unemployment; incursions on the equal rights of Chicanos, other oppressed minorities, and women; weakening of job safety standards; and destruction of the environment.

The articles in this book put forward a strategy for uniting

Chicanos and their allies to fight back against these and future attacks. They elaborate a program of demands based on the day-to-day needs and aspirations of the Chicano community. This transitional program is grounded in the reality that Chicanos, as well as other oppressed national minorities, have been systematically denied the benefits and rights conquered by the revolution of 1776 and the Civil War—the first two American revolutions. This program is also based on the fact that the drive by the Chicano people to seize and enjoy the democratic conquests of these revolutions is integrally linked to the fight of all working people to overturn the economic system established by these two revolutions, to wrest control over their lives and destinies from the hands of the ruling rich, and to change the priorities of society so that its resources are used to satisfy the needs of all of humanity rather than the profit hunger of the minority presently in power.

This intertwining of the needs of Chicanos and other oppressed national minorities with those of the working class as a whole give the coming American revolution its unique character. The third American revolution will be a combined one: that is, it will combine the solution of the problems created by capitalist exploitation with the elimination of the national oppression of Chicanos, Blacks, and other minorities—a problem left unresolved following the first two revolutions in this country.

Because of this special interrelation, Chicanos along with other minorities are thrust into the vanguard of the coming American revolution. The struggles of Chicanos in the social, economic and political arenas, *because* of their position as an oppressed nationality on the one hand, and as one of the most exploited layers of the working class on the other, can propel the working class as a whole into motion.

The analyses contained in the following contributions provide a powerful rejoinder to those who claim that the struggle of Chicanos against their own special oppression is a diversion and an obstacle to the struggle of the working class as a whole. These detractors of the Chicano movement fail to grasp the dynamic of this interrelationship, and thus, the dynamic of the coming American socialist revolution.

This book also answers those who maintain that Chicano liberation can be won by relying on a section of the American capitalist class through supporting their political representatives—the Democratic and Republican parties. On the contrary, it is the *dependence* on the parties representing those responsible for the second class status of Chicanos that retards the fight for Chicano liberation. The significance of the development of local and state Raza Unida parties—Chicano political parties independent of and in opposition to the Democratic and Republican parties—is discussed at length in this book. These parties are the first steps by a superexploited section of the working class to break from the stranglehold of the twin parties of their oppression and exploitation. As such, the Raza Unida parties are the most advanced organizations to emerge out of the Chicano struggle, and they provide a powerful example to the working class as a whole. In the pages of the *Militant* and the new Spanish-language biweekly magazine, *Perspectiva Mundial,** the SWP supports and helps to popularize the development of these parties as a step toward the construction of a mass Chicano political party. This position stems from the SWP's understanding of the need for political independence of the working class and its allies.

The materials included in this book are not meant to be the last word on the questions of strategy and program that confront Chicanos, but should be seen as a contribution to an evolving debate and discussion necessary to clarify the place of the fight for Chicano liberation in the overall class struggle. *The Politics of Chicano Liberation* expresses the point of view of revolutionary socialism, in the traditions of Marx, Engels, Lenin, and Trotsky. It does not claim to put forward or argue all aspects of every question in one short volume. Our analysis is basically a guide to a living struggle that will bring forth new battles, new challenges and new leaders. It is hoped that this book will help further the development of a revolutionary leadership that can claim the tools of Marxism as its own and apply them to advance the cause of Chicano liberation.

Olga Rodríguez
June 1977

*Subscriptions to the *Militant* are $2 for twelve weeks; 14 Charles Lane, New York NY 10014. *Perspectiva Mundial* is $10 for one year; P.O. Box 314, Village Station, New York NY 10014.

The Forging of an Oppressed Nationality

by Antonio Camejo

This article originally appeared as a contribution to the Socialist Workers Party discussion bulletin in 1971.

The following historical sketch in intended only as a schematic overview of some of the main events which led to the forging of the Chicano people into a distinct oppressed nationality. Nor does it attempt to present a rounded analysis of major events such as the Mexican-American War. As such, it should not be viewed as a complete Marxist history of the Chicano people. That is yet to be written, and this is just one small step in that direction.

The Spanish Conquest of Mexico

The Chicano people have their origins in the racial and cultural mixture of Spaniards with the native populations of what is now Mexico and the agricultural Pueblo Indians of what is now the southwestern part of the United States.

The Spanish conquest of Mexico beginning in 1519, and the exploration of what is now California, Arizona, Colorado, New Mexico, and Texas predate the arrival of the Pilgrims by almost a century. By 1630 the Spanish had founded twenty-five missions and a series of settlements in New Mexico. From New Mexico settlements spread into Arizona and California. While Juan Bautista de Anza was exploring San Francisco Bay, the European colonists on the eastern seaboard were celebrating the signing of the Declaration of Independence.

Between 1769 and 1823, the Spanish had established in California a string of twenty-one missions, four presidial towns (military garrisons), two pueblos (San José and Los Angeles), and a number of settlements in Texas and Arizona. By 1848 there were approximately 75,000 Spanish-speaking settlers (predominantly mestizos, people of Indian-Spanish stock) in these northern provinces of Mexico; 7,500 in California; 1,000 in Arizona; 60,000 in New Mexico; and 5,000 in Texas. There were approximately 250,000 native inhabitants in the same area.

While the British colonized the eastern seaboard with large numbers of settlers, the Spanish conquerors were few in number and predominantly male. The British drove the native population they encountered off the land. Later, as Anglo-American capitalism pushed westward, its rulers developed a conscious policy of genocide against the Native American population and forced the survivors onto reservations.

Unlike the eastern seaboard settlements, Spanish colonial society was built on the backs of the indigenous inhabitants. The Spanish discovered a people one stage beyond those that the British found along the East Coast. The Aztec society, based on the cultivation of corn, was in the middle stages of barbarism. The Spanish were in a period of transition from feudalism to capitalism. The inevitable and irreconcilable clash produced by the meeting of these agents of European class society with the collectivist societies of the Aztecs and other indigenous peoples of Mexico resulted not only in a new race, the mestizo, but also in combined economic forms. Early colonial society in Mexico was as much feudal as it was bourgeois. Colonial and postcolonial society was characterized by the exploitation of precapitalist modes of production (serfdom, slavery, debt peonage, sharecropping) for the benefit of the rising capitalist system.

The conquest of the Aztecs and of other native peoples living in what became the Republic of Mexico resulted in their decimation. Disease, slavery, overwork in the fields and in the mines, starvation caused by the expropriation and export of agricultural produce, and the brutal repression against all resistance to the conquest took their toll. It is estimated that Tenochtitlán (Mexico City) had upwards of 300,000 inhabitants and that several million Indians populated the Valley of Mexico. In 1646 this population reached a low point of 1,250,000.

Revolts broke out throughout the colonial period. A revolt by the Pueblo Indians in 1680 drove the Spanish and mestizos out of

New Mexico. It was not until twelve years later that the area was resettled. In 1848 those who dominated major sections of the provinces of northern Mexico were neither Mexicans nor Anglo-Americans. They were the nomadic Apaches and other hunters and food gatherers who resisted not only the Spanish and the mestizo settlers but also the Anglo invasion of the area.

The frontier settlements of northern Mexico were separated from the central seat of power in Mexico City by large belts of desert and hostility of the native peoples who controlled the deserts separating New Mexico from California and isolating New Mexico from the settlements in Texas. With the opening of the Santa Fe trail in 1820, residents of New Mexico could trade more easily with Saint Louis than with Chihuahua in northern Mexico. These geographical factors, as well as the resistance of those Indians who refused to be conquered, led to a certain isolation of Mexico's northernmost provinces from the central administration of the weak *criolle* (Mexican-born Spaniards) bourgeoisie. This encouraged the territorial ambitions of both the slavocracy and northeastern capitalists in the United States, who viewed these territories as easy prey.

The ability of Mexico to govern its northern provinces was further weakened during the ten-year struggle for national independence in which 500,000 of its citizens lost their lives. Although formal independence from Spain was achieved in 1821, the *criolle* bourgeoisie merely replaced the Spanish administration, leaving the conditions of the masses unaltered. Independence was soon followed by the Spanish invasion of Tampico in 1829, a short-lived French blockade of Veracruz in 1838, and secession of Yucatán from 1839 to 1843, and was marked by unstable govermental regimes up to 1851.

The U.S. Conquest of Northern Mexico

The introduction of the cotton gin in the late 1790s greatly increased the desire of the southern slavocracy to open up new land to exploit. This drive for territorial expansion led to the Louisiana Purchase from the French in 1803, the purchase of Florida from Spain in 1819, and the eventual clash with Mexico over the twelve-year period from 1836 to 1848.

A further factor propelled the slave system westward. The intense production of cotton as a single cash crop quickly impoverished the soil of the South, resulting in lower yields. Since the Compromise of 1820 prohibited slavery from moving northwest, the Mexican province of Texas, which was larger than France and well suited for cotton, was a logical area for expansion.

As early as 1825, President John Quincy Adams attempted to purchase the Texas province from Mexico. When Mexico refused, other means were employed. The southern planters who dominated the U.S. federal government encouraged the settling of Texas by Anglo-Americans with the hope that they would outnumber the small Mexican population and create enough difficulties for Mexico so that it would relinquish control to the United States. After initially issuing land grants to such settlers, Mexico became alarmed at the rapid growth of the Anglo population and the violation of the conditions stipulated in the grants. In 1830 a Mexican government decree prohibited further colonization of Texas by Anglo-Americans and called for collection of custom duties along the Louisiana border.

The Anglo-American Texans, who were legally Mexican citizens, refused to submit to the authority of the Mexican government and maintained slavery. They set up the Independent Republic of Texas in 1836. This led to the sending of Mexican troops into Texas, resulting in the attack on the Alamo by General Santa Anna and the subsequent defeat of Santa Anna by the army of Sam Houston. By that time Anglo-American settlers outnumbered the Mexicanos by 6 to 1. The slavocracy looked forward to immediately annexing Texas to the United States with the idea of carving six slave states out of the immense territory. But divisions within the U.S. ruling classes delayed annexation until 1845.

The main issue of the presidential campaign of 1844 was the annexation of Texas, with the Democratic Party running James Polk in favor, and the Whigs running Henry Clay in moderate opposition to annexation. The victory of the Democrats, who represented the southern planters, guaranteed annexation.

But the plans and desires of the slavocracy went beyond Texas. President Polk was intent on provoking Mexico into a war which would end in the conquest of all of Mexico. The Democratic Party convention, meeting in New York State in 1844, resolved: "That the title of the Mexican government is a title by conquest from those who held it by conquest. If we took it and held it by the same title, they could not complain. Their title is legal; and our title would also be legal." The chairman of the Senate Committee on Foreign Relations stated in 1848 that the Mexicans could be removed to reservations in the same manner as the United States had subjugated the native North Americans.

The northern capitalists opposed adding Texas as another slave state and feared the enhanced political weight of a strengthened slavocracy expanding south into Mexico. But they favored provoking a war with Mexico to gain the commercially valuable harbors of California. The commander of the United States exploring expedition to the Pacific prior to 1845 praised the commercial possibilities of the West Coast, stating that it could easily fall into the hands of "the Anglo-Norman race . . . having none to enter into rivalry with it but the indolent inhabitants of warm climates. . . ."

The ideological justification for this expansionism was Manifest Destiny. President Polk expressed the desires of the U.S. ruling class in the following terms: "Our union is a federation of independent states whose policy is peace with each other and all the world. To enlarge its limits is to extend the dominions of peace over additional territories and increasing millions." But the expression of this expansionism was not merely limited to a particular view of the American nation. The racist ideology of the ruling class, both North and South, was perhaps best expressed by a northern capitalist, Commodore Stockton, who commanded the U.S. assault in California during the war with Mexico: "I will not attempt to impeach or defend what I believe to be the inevitable destiny of my country and of my race. . . . I am unwilling to say to my countrymen that you shall go no farther east or west or north or south. I am unwilling that the Anglo-American race shall perpetually recoil from any given boundary and that any portion of this continent not now in their possession shall forever be impenetrable to their civilization, enterprise and industry."

The war began in 1846, and during its course the United States defeated Mexico's armies and occupied Mexico City. The Democratic administration favored taking all of Mexico, but was stopped short by opposition in Congress. The government negotiator completed the Treaty of Guadalupe Hidalgo on February 2, 1848, against the orders of Polk. The treaty was subsequently ratified by the Senate giving the United States one-half of Mexico's national territory, an area larger than France and Germany combined. In addition to Texas the newly won U.S. territory encompassed what are now the states of California,

Nevada, Utah, New Mexico, Arizona, part of Wyoming, and the western part of Colorado.

Mexico attempted to include a provision prohibiting slavery in the ceded area but this was rejected by the United States. Mexico was paid $15 million for the entire area. The Mesilla Valley (Gadsden Purchase), was added in 1853.

Besides formalizing the military conquest, the Treaty of Guadalupe Hidalgo also guaranteed certain rights to the conquered Mexican inhabitants. Article VIII stated:

"Mexicans now established in territories previously belonging to Mexico, and which remain for the future within the limits of the United States, as defined by the present treaty, shall be free to continue where they now reside, or to remove at any time to the Mexican Republic, retaining the property which they possess in the said territories. . . .

"In the said territories, property of every kind, now belonging to Mexicans not established there, shall be inviolably respected. The present owners, the heirs of these, and all Mexicans who may hereafter acquire said property by contract, shall enjoy with respect to it guarantees equally ample as if the same belonged to citizens of the United States."

Article IX guaranteed to those who became citizens (automatic one year from the date of the treaty, unless an individual specifically chose to remain a Mexican citizen) "enjoyment of all the rights of citizens of the United States, according to the principles of the Constitution," and also "the free enjoyment of their liberty and property, and secure in the free exercise of their religion without restriction."

Every one of these guarantees has been systematically violated since that day.

New Mexico and Arizona

With the end of the Civil War the United States government concentrated its military forces on crushing the Indians, including those in the territory of Arizona and New Mexico. In order to keep the southern routes to California open for commerce and to consolidate its hold over this former Mexican territory, the U.S. Army systematically destroyed the flocks, fields, and orchards of the Navajos, forcing their surrender and removal to reservations. The Apaches and Comanches, severely reduced in numbers and area, were driven into the worst desert or rugged mountain areas and were finally defeated and captured.

This had the temporary effect of permitting a brief expansion of the Mexicano settlements, particularly in New Mexico and Arizona. But this process was cut short by the expanding Anglo cattle ranchers and farmers who encroached on the Mexicano farmers and sheepherders. The trade which developed between Santa Fe and Saint Louis had gradually opened up New Mexico and Arizona to the influence of eastern capital. The establishment of the railroads along the old trails to Santa Fe and then on to California by 1885, eclipsed the trade of Mexicano caravans.

Along with the railroads came the growth of capital-intensive mining operations which shifted from gold to silver and then to copper, displacing Mexicano miners through competition where it was not done through outright fraud and violence. By 1900 mining was predominantly mechanized and controlled by eastern capitalists using a Mexicano labor force. Anglo capitalists extended their railroad and mining interests into northern Mexico itself. By 1910 Guggenheim had a virtual monopoly of the metallurgical industry in Mexico and U.S. interests dominated the railroads there.

The railroads of the Southwest were built mainly by Mexicano labor. After 1880 up to 70 percent of section crews and 90 percent of the extra gangs on the principal western lines were Mexicanos. The present Chicano settlements of Chicago and Kansas City grew out of railroad labor camps.

California

A new rich lode of gold was discovered in California almost immediately after the signing of the Treaty of Guadalupe Hidalgo in 1848. Mexicans had been successfully mining gold between Los Angeles and Santa Cruz a decade before James W. Marshall made his famous discovery.

The *Californios,* as the Mexican inhabitants of that former part of Mexico referred to themselves, lost no time in applying their mining knowledge to the rich deposits. By 1848 1,300 out of the approximately 7,500 Mexican population were engaged in gold mining. By the end of 1848 there were already some 4,000 Anglo miners. The news of the new discovery of gold brought some 8,000 Mexicans from Sonora into California along with 5,000 South

Americans, mainly Chileans and Peruvians. But the largest influx was of Anglo-Americans, who by the end of 1849 numbered 80,000.

The period from 1849 to 1860 was one of violence, fraud, and intimidation against Spanish-speaking miners, ranchers, and farmers by Anglo miners who considered them to be something less than human beings, an attitude reflecting the ideology of the capitalist and slaveholder ruling classes in Washington, now in control of California. Whippings, brandings, ear croppings, and lynchings were commonplace occurrences for Mexicano miners who dared to defend their claims as guaranteed by the Treaty of Guadalupe Hidalgo.

When California became a state in 1850, the state legislature wasted no time in levying the notorious foreign miners' license tax law of 1850, which was used as a pretext to drive Mexicanos, Chileans, and Peruvians out of their mine claims.

From 1850 to 1900, the Anglo settlers, merchants, and their politicians and lawyers expropriated almost the entire propertied class of *Californios*. (This class was predominantly of Spanish blood and light-skinned.) Those who did not lose their lands were reduced to small holdings. Toward the end of the 1800s the Mexicano population was in retreat, the distinction between *Californios* and *Cholos* (the poor working masses of predominantly Indian blood) all but wiped out, and a racist Anglo majority firmly entrenched. This point was not reached, however, without a fight. Guerrilla bands developed during the 1850s which tried to hold back the Anglo invasion. But the forces of occupation were overwhelming.

The expropriation of *Tejano* (Mexican Texan) landowners by Anglos proceeded in a similar fashion. In California, New Mexico, and Texas many of the *ricos* (wealthy Mexican landowners) collaborated with the Anglo invaders but to little avail. They too were either expropriated or driven out of business by a combination of Anglo lawyers and unfavorable economic conditions. Succeeding generations of these families were driven into the working class. The tremendous wealth derived from the mines and lands stolen from Mexico and then from the Mexican owners themselves, played an important part in the financing of eastern capitalist expansion.

Agribusiness and "Merchants of Labor"

As early as the 1890s Mexicanos were working the cotton fields of East Texas. By 1910 cotton was spreading into central Texas, creating a need for cheap labor. Certain conditions in Mexico created the labor supply to meet that need. The recession of 1907 generated a large amount of unemployment which encouraged the beginnings of migration from Mexico. With the start of the Mexican revolution in 1910 this migration was greatly accelerated.

The First World War also created an expanding need in the United States for agricultural produce and textiles. During the first three decades of the twentieth century, one million Mexicans crossed into the United States, primarily into Texas and California. The passage of the Immigration Act of 1924, which reduced European immigration, increased demand for Mexicano workers, who moved as far north as Detroit, as far east as Pittsburgh, and into Alaskan canneries.

Prior to 1924 the contract-labor law of 1885 forced growers to recruit labor illegally. Labor smugglers went into Mexico to recruit workers. On bringing them across the border they would be sold to a labor contractor who would then sell the workers for 50 cents to $1.00 a head, to a grower or railroad or mine employer. Carey McWilliams in *North From Mexico* described the handling of these workers:

"Shipments of workers en route to employers were often kept locked up at night, in barns, warehouses, and corrals, with armed guards posted to prevent their theft. Crews of imported Mexicans were marched through the streets of San Antonio under armed guard in broad daylight and, in Gonzales County, workers who attempted to breach their contracts were chained to posts and guarded by men with shotguns."

By 1929 the Southwest was producing 40 percent of the nation's supply of vegetables, fruit, and truck crops with a labor force that was from 65 percent to 85 percent Mexican. The sugar beet industry in Colorado alone produced more profits than all the gold and silver ever mined in that state. Agribusiness was not alone in recognizing the profit that could result from a cheap source of labor. Some workers went directly from central Mexico, as well as from Texas, to Midwest industrial centers where they were employed in steel mills, packing plants, auto factories, and tanneries. The pressure from the sugar beet industry, the Texas Emigrant Agent Law of 1929, and the depression brought this movement to a halt.

Contrary to the myth of their docility, Mexicano workers began organizing as early as 1883 in Texas. Strikes occurred throughout the country before World War I and after, but they were almost invariably met with violence and deportation. Many of these deported workers then became union organizers in Mexico. Some, including IWW members, played a role in the famous Cananea miners' strike in Sonora, Mexico, in 1906, a date marking the start of the Mexican labor movement. During the depression years in the 1930s, tens of thousands of Mexicanos were forced by the U.S. government to repatriate to get them off the welfare rolls. Many were from families who had lived in the United States for generations.

World War II

The start of the Second World War brought about dramatic changes among the Mexicano population of the United States. With the expanded war production many farm workers were drawn into the cities and into basic industry. Although this did not create a shortage of labor in agriculture, the growers feared that elimination of the large surplus labor pool would drive wages up and create conditions more favorable for unionization. Also, competition with industrial wage rates would mean a lowering of profit.

The growers convinced the Roosevelt administration to negotiate a contract with Mexico for the importation of farm workers, as an emergency war measure. This Bracero Program amounted to a direct subsidy of agribusiness which was already garnering huge profits. Under the plan, the U.S. government paid out $120 million to import a total of about 400,000 Mexicans between 1943 and 1947. They were restricted to agriculture, although a special arrangement was made for 80,000 of them to work as section hands and maintenance workers on the railroads at low wages.

The war resulted in an increasing urbanization of La Raza and further proletarianization of their ranks. The war, however, had a further effect. Many Mexicanos believed that service in the armed forces was a means of gaining full rights as citizens of the United States. Another important aspect of the war experience was that, while Afro-Americans were in separate, all-Black units, Mexicanos were not segregated. This did not mean freedom from discrimination and racist practices, but it was an improvement over the repressive conditions experienced in the barrios of East Los Angeles and the fields of Texas and California.

The so-called Zoot Suit Riots of 1943 were the most notorious examples of overt racism and brutality toward Mexicanos in this period. Following on the heels of the internment in concentration camps of the Japanese-Americans in 1942, and the hysterical campaign against nonwhite peoples which accompanied the expropriation of the Japanese-Americans, the Los Angeles press began a campaign against youth known as "Pachucos" (identified by the zoot suits many young Mexicanos then wore). The Hearst press and the *Los Angeles Times* played on all the racist attitudes of the Anglo population, including the local police theory that Mexicanos were biologically predisposed to violence and crime. They whipped up an atmosphere which led to a week of vicious attacks by Anglo servicemen on Mexicano youth especially, but also on Black youth in Los Angeles.

The events in Los Angeles were followed by similar attacks on Black and Mexicano communities elsewhere, from Beaumont, Texas, to Detroit, Michigan. The international embarrassment these incidents caused Washington finally forced President Roosevelt to intervene. Most serious to the ruling class was the possibility of Mexico cutting off the Bracero Program in protest. Roosevelt's refusal to act swiftly to defend the victims of these racist attacks is one more item in the long list of the crimes of the Democratic Party.

The impact of U.S. capitalist propaganda about "liberating oppressed peoples" from fascism and colonialism, however, was great. Mexicano GIs returning from years of the imperialist slaughter were expecting respect and full rights. They found quite a different situation, however. They were discriminated against as before, and were even excluded from groups such as the American Legion and other veterans' organizations. They were still considered "greasers," "dirty Mexicans."

One postwar incident helped focus the resentment and bitterness of La Raza. The family of a Texas Chicano war hero was refused a plot in a Corpus Christi cemetery for their son. The national and international embarrassment to the ruling class caused President Truman to provide burial for the soldier in Arlington National Cemetery. But the lesson was not lost on returning veterans, who founded their own organizations, such as the GI Forum, organized in 1948 in Corpus Christi, Texas. While the Forum stated that one of its objectives was to "preserve and defend the United States of America from all enemies," it also proposed to "secure and protect for all veterans and their families, regardless of race, creed or color, the privileges invested in them by the Constitution and laws of our country." In less than a year, there were more than 100 GI Forum chapters throughout the Southwest.

Another such organization was the Unity League, organized in southern California. Composed primarily of veterans and workers, the Unity League participated in electoral activity, running candidates of their own and electing a city councilman in Chino, California, in 1946. This victory encouraged others to run for office. Ed Roybal, a veteran, ran for Los Angeles city council as an independent. Although he lost, an organization grew out of his campaign called the Community Service Organization (CSO), which was at first composed solely of World War II veterans and was then expanded to include first their wives and later others from the broader community. In 1949 Roybal ran again and won with the support of the CSO. With the advent of the cold war, Roybal quickly moved to the right, into the Democratic Party, where he has remained to this day. The CSO meanwhile became involved in a series of community activities and civil rights fights.

César Chávez, leader of the farm workers' union, gained much of his political experience as an organizer for and one time director of the CSO. After it conducted successful voter registration and education drives (in 1960, the CSO registered 137,000 Chicanos to vote, 95 percent of whom voted for John F. Kennedy), the AFL-CIO began giving the CSO financial assistance to expand their work. In recent years, however, the organization has been declining in both membership and influence and has tended to oppose the new rise of Chicano militancy.

Thousands of the returning World War II veterans took advantage of the GI Bill of Rights to get a high school and college education, to buy homes, and to set up small businesses. By 1956, 2 percent of the professionals in Los Angeles County had Spanish surnames. Organizations reflecting the small but growing number of white-collar workers and professionals sprang up during the 1950s. The Council of Mexican-American Affairs

(CMAA) in Los Angeles, attempting to bring together various community organizations, gave birth to a special education committee which raised the issue of special programs to meet the needs of Chicano students. The Association of Mexican-American Educators (AMAE), founded in 1965, continued this work, also helping to elect Julian Nava to the Los Angeles school board in 1967. In 1959, the Mexican-American Political Association (MAPA) was organized as the first Mexican-American group in the postwar period to proclaim itself political. It was built around the Democratic Party successes of 1958 when several Chicanos were elected to office in California.

The Second World War, then, saw increased urbanization of La Raza, proletarianization of its ranks, and the development of a small layer of professionals. Organizations reflecting these changes appeared in the late 1940s and 1950s and helped set the stage for the resurgence of militancy in the decade of the 1960s.

1968 high school blowout in East Los Angeles

Crystal City, Texas, 1970

National Chicano Moratorium to End the War in Vietnam, August 29, 1970

The Struggle for Chicano Liberation

This resolution was adopted at the Twenty-fourth National Convention of the SWP in August 1971.

For many years the Chicano people were considered the silent or forgotten minority, or referred to anonymously as one of the other oppressed nationalities. The plight of Chicanos as an oppressed people was not in the public spotlight.

This situation was to change dramatically in the mid- and late-1960s as an independent movement developed in response to the specific oppression of the Chicano people, which had a dynamic and revolutionary logic of its own. The Afro-American and student movements were joined by a movement of those who had called themselves Mexican-Americans, Hispanos, Latin Americans, Spanish-speaking. Part of the nationalist dynamic of this development was a new self-image. Terms of self-description like *La Raza* and *Chicano* gained greater acceptance, reflecting a new pride and dignity, a new determination to struggle for equal rights, for a better life, for liberation.

This resolution describes the roots of this nationalist awakening and traces the developments which led to the new rise of Chicano militancy and combativity in the 1960s. It outlines the current stage of the struggle, the propsects for independent political action, some initial components of a transitional program for Chicano liberation, and the tasks of the Socialist Workers Party in this important movement.

Roots of Chicano Nationalism

The conquest by the United States of the northern half of Mexico in the mid-nineteenth century resulted not only in the incorporation of a huge land mass into the territory of the United States but the incorporation of the Mexican population as well. These people and their descendants, set apart by race, language, and culture, were not assimilated as full and equal citizens, whatever formal guarantees were made to the contrary. Instead, they were systematically discriminated against as a people, and forged by expanding American capitalism into a distinct oppressed nationality. Subsequent immigration from Mexico swelled the ranks of this oppressed people.

Except for Native Americans, Chicanos suffer the highest unemployment, the lowest per capita income, the worst education, the highest functional illiteracy rate, the highest death rate, occupy the most dilapidated and overcrowded housing, and have less political representation in local, state, or national government than any other nationality in the population of the Southwest and perhaps in the nation.

The 1970 census put the "Spanish-surnamed" population at approximately 9 million, about 5 million of whom are Chicanos. The real figures are assumed to be much higher, with estimates by scholars of 10 million Chicanos at a minimum. More than 80 percent of Chicanos live in the five southwestern states of California, Texas, Arizona, New Mexico, and Colorado. The rest are spread out over the entire country from Florida to Alaska, from New Jersey to Illinois.

By 1960 La Raza was as urbanized as the Anglo population. Eighty percent of Chicanos in the Southwest live in cities. Most of them are workers. For example, over 30,000 of the 90,000 members of the United Steelworkers of America in the western states are Chicanos. Sixteen percent of the Chicano labor force are farm workers, many of whom live in urban areas.

Of the total elementary and secondary student population in the Southwest, 17 percent are Chicanos and 10 percent are Blacks, yet only 4 percent of the teachers and only 3 percent of the principals are Chicanos. There are approximately twenty Anglo students for every Anglo teacher in the Southwest, thirty-nine Black students for every Black teacher, and one hundred and twenty Chicano students for every Chicano teacher.

The only school jobs in which Chicanos are proportionately represented, in school districts with 10 percent Chicanos or more, are custodians (28 percent) and teacher's aides (34 percent). While the median educational grades attended for whites is twelve years it is only eight years for Chicanos.

It is clear that language plays a critical role in maintaining the oppression of the Chicano people. According to the 1970 census, 50 percent of Spanish-surnamed people stated that Spanish is their primary language. The overwhelming majority of Chicano youth enter the schools speaking Spanish. By the time they drop out or graduate they have been partly or completely stripped of their first language without attaining a proficiency in English equal to that of Anglos. Thus they leave school with a linguistic handicap.

The suppression of the Spanish language in the schools is one of the most insidious forms of the oppression of the Chicano people. The use of Spanish by Chicano children in the schools has been restricted or banned even in states where prohibitive legislation has been repealed. Through attempting to obliterate the Spanish language, the capitalist ruling class hoped to strip Chicanos of their cultural identity and history in the same manner that the slave masters stripped the African slaves of their languages and identities. While this objective was never fully achieved, the damage done to Chicano students and their ability to learn has been dramatic. Racist textbooks and teachers and irrelevant materials have created a 50 percent "push out" (so-called drop out) rate from the predominantly Chicano high schools of East Los Angeles. In Texas the figure for Chicano push outs is 47 percent. Functional illiteracy among Chicanos is seven times that for Anglos and twice that for Afro-Americans. In Texas 50 percent of the Chicano heads of households are functionally illiterate. The use of linguistically and culturally biased intelligence tests has led to placing Chicano students in California in classes for the mentally retarded at a rate 250 percent out of proportion to their numbers in the population.

Inferior education, a linguistic handicap, and racist hiring practices force Chicanos into the worst low-paying jobs. The per capita income for Chicano workers in 1959 was 58 percent of that of white workers. Since then, the income gap between whites and Chicanos has widened. In Texas 34 percent of the Chicano families live in poverty, in New Mexico it is 30 percent, 22 percent in Colorado, 21 percent in Arizona, 15 percent in California.

While, in 1960, 14 percent of the Anglo work force were classified as professionals, only 4 percent of the Chicanos were in the same category, and 6 percent of the Blacks. Chicanos suffer four times the rate of crowding in housing compared to whites.

It is the combination of all these factors which gives Chicanos a higher incidence of tuberculosis, infant mortality, and chronic diseases and illnesses associated with malnutrition, poverty, and lack of medical care. For example, the life expectancy of Chicano farm workers is forty-eight years.

*   *   *

The expansion and consolidation of American capitalism was carried out through the subjugation of various peoples, including the Chicanos, and their incorporation into its structure as oppressed nationalities. This national oppression within the borders of the United States has benefited and continues to benefit the ruling class in many ways and is essential to its continued rule. It has divided the working class and increased its stratification, created pools of cheap labor and detachments of the industrial reserve army, and provided workers for the most difficult, dangerous, or seasonal and low-paying jobs. White racism, the ideological justification for such national oppression, is used demagogically by the rulers to divert white workers away from struggling against their capitalist class enemy and toward supporting the oppression of Chicanos and other oppressed nationalities both within the borders of the United States and beyond.

The ruling class will never grant freedom to oppressed nationalities, including La Raza. The national liberation of the Chicano people can be won only in the process of the socialist revolution, which will have a combined character: a social revolution by the working class to establish its own state power, combined with a revolution by the oppressed nationalities for their self-determination. The predominantly proletarian composition of the Chicano people indicates that they will be in the forefront of the revolutionary struggle of the working class as a whole, as well as fighting alongside other oppressed nationalities for their national self-determination.

Rise of the Chicano Nationalist Movement

Many of the developments which led to the worldwide youth radicalization of the 1960s also affected the Chicano people and helped facilitate the emergence of a new generation of militant young Chicanos.

The colonial revolution showed that peoples long oppressed could rise up and win their freedom. The Cuban revolution especially had an impact in the Chicano community.

The first mass reflection of the colonial revolution in the United States was the movement of the Afro-American people. The struggles of this oppressed nationality shook up the political equilibrium, helped to inspire the youth radicalization, and served as a model for subsequent insurgent movements it helped set into motion. The student movement, the antiwar movement, the Chicano movement, and more recently the women's liberation movement, owe much to the initiating role of the Black movement, the lessons of its successful and unsuccessful strategies and tactics, and the experiences of Black organizations and leaderships.

The Chicano movement has benefited from the experiences of these movements, and, in turn, it has taught lessons in its own right, surged ahead in some aspects, and now provides examples especially for the Black movement.

Two efforts were begun in 1962 that were to influence the initial stages of the new Chicano movement and inspire subsequent developments. These were the farm workers' movement and the land-grant organizing efforts led respectively by César Chávez and Reies López Tijerina.

The Farm Workers

César Chávez resigned from his position of leadership in the Community Service Organization in 1961 when conservative elements blocked his efforts to use the CSO to support the struggles of Chicano farm workers. The following year he formed the Farm Workers Association, which was to become a social movement, a union of farm workers that could fight for collective bargaining with the rich growers, but would also deal with medical, language, and other problems faced by farm workers.

In 1965 the association joined forces with a Filipino farm workers' group to form the United Farm Workers Organizing Committee, based in California. The expiration of the Bracero Program at the end of 1964 (although it partially continued under the Green Card program) had created a new opportunity to organize farm workers with less likelihood that strikes could be broken by the massive importation of Mexican labor. A strike of grape workers began in the fall of 1965 and, though it won some initial concessions, it was necessary to carry out a protracted grape boycott campaign before substantial victories were won and consolidated.

The organizing efforts and achievements in California had a major impact upon the barrios and farm-labor camps around the country and led to similar developments in Arizona, Texas, Washington, Colorado, and other states.

It was *La Huelga* (the strike), together with the land-grant movement in New Mexico, that first forced this forgotten minority into the public eye and proclaimed the emergence of a new civil and human rights movement. The migrant laborers, who were said by racists to be naturally endowed for such stoop labor because they were "built low to the ground," were challenging racist stereotypes and asserting their humanity. Chicanos shouting *"Huelga!"* and *"Viva La Causa!"* and demanding *"Justicia y Libertad!"* added another powerful element to the struggles of the oppressed and exploited.

The farm workers' movement has been led for the most part by pacifist reformists like Chávez, who supports liberal Democrats. Nevertheless this movement has had an independent, nationalist dynamic which has helped set other sectors of La Raza into motion.

This independent dynamic has been incomplete and blunted by the refusal of the Chávez leadership to break politically with the Democratic Party and initiate an independent Chicano party. Such a development is a necessary step for the success of the farm workers' struggle. It could result in rapid electoral victories in the cities and towns of the rich farm country in the valleys of California, and in other states, where Chicanos are a majority. These victories in turn would give fresh impetus to unionization efforts, the fight for higher wages, better conditions, health and child care, and other struggles.

The growth of La Raza Unida Party in 1970 and 1971 has exerted considerable pressure on the farm workers' movement to embark on the road of independent Chicano political action. This may be seen in Chávez's recent statement in favor of La Raza Unida candidates. If the farm workers' union should begin to stray from the Meany-approved subordination of the labor movement to the Democratic Party, the AFL-CIO bureaucracy can be expected to exert considerable pressure on the farm workers by withdrawing financial and other support.

The Land-Grant Movement

In violation of the provisions of the Treaty of Guadalupe Hidalgo, which ended the U.S. war with Mexico in 1848, the property of the Mexican inhabitants of what is now the Southwest U.S. was not respected.

Reies López Tijerina investigated the original land-grant titles and exposed the processes by which they were stolen. The Alianza Federal de Mercedes (Federal Alliance of Land Grants) was formed in 1962 in New Mexico to publicize the claims of the *"Indo-Hispanos"* to the land now occupied by Anglos and by the National Forest Service.

A series of events beginning in 1966 brought the Alianza to public attention nationally. A march from Albuquerque to Santa Fe with petitions to the governor of New Mexico and the president of the United States was followed by attempts to occupy parts of National Forest lands in the fall of 1966 and the summer of 1967. This was answered by military force and frame-up charges against Alianza leaders.

Included in the program of the Alianza was the idea of internationalizing their struggle by appealing to the United Nations and Cuba to recognize their claims to the land and their right to establish an independent republic based on the land grants.

The Alianza participated in a New Politics formation, the People's Constitutional Party of New Mexico, during the 1968 elections, running Tijerina for governor. They, along with the Crusade for Justice of Denver and the farm workers' union, joined the Southern Christian Leadership Conference's Poor People's March on Washington in 1968. Tijerina and other Alianza militants, after frame-up trials, were imprisoned and the Alianza has declined.

With Chicanos constituting more than one-third of New Mexico's population, and a majority in some areas, considerable potential exists for building an independent Chicano party there, although no such efforts have been undertaken thus far.

Crusade for Justice

An urban civil rights and cultural movement called the Crusade for Justice was formed in Denver, Colorado, in the mid-1960s. While located solely in Denver, the Crusade's influence was to be more widely felt as its principal spokesman, Rodolfo "Corky" González, a former official of the Democratic Party, emerged as one of the central leaders in the Chicano movement.

The Crusade for Justice organized and supported high school strikes, demonstrations against police brutality, and legal cases in behalf of Chicanos framed up by the police. It also supported mass actions against the Vietnam War.

One of the most important roles played by the Crusade has been organizing the Chicano Youth Liberation conferences. The 1969 and 1970 conferences brought together large numbers of Chicano youth from the Southwest, the Northwest, and the Midwest, as well as some Puerto Rican youth from the Midwest and East Coast. Out of the first conference came *El Plan Espiritual de Aztlán* (The Spiritual Plan of Aztlán), a program for the mass mobilization of Chicanos for community control. The Plan of Aztlán raised the concept that the liberation of the "Mestizo Nation" would ultimately require "a nation autonomously free, culturally, socially, economically, and politically." The formation of an independent Chicano party was projected "since the two-party system is the same animal with two heads that feeds from the same trough."

The second Chicano youth conference (1970) represented a further step forward for those forces who supported a mass-action perspective and the formation of an independent Chicano political party. Following the conference, the Crusade for Justice and other Chicanos launched the Colorado Raza Unida Party.

The Chicano Student Movement

The schools have been a place where Chicano youth have been politicized by many of the factors that fueled the international youth radicalization, as well as by many specific grievances. By the 1960s the number of Chicano youth in the high schools had dramatically increased. There are approximately two million Spanish-surnamed elementary and secondary school students in the United States, 70 percent of them in the Southwest. More Chicano students than before are now going on to college, but not in the same proportion as the rest of the population.

The Chicano student movement developed to combat oppressive school conditions. High school and elementary students were prohibited from using Spanish in the classroom or on the school grounds; the true history of the Chicano people was not taught;

Anglo principals and teachers directly and indirectly expressed their racist concepts and attitudes; and Chicano students not pushed out of the schools were tracked into vocational rather than academic courses, often into the army rather than college. Students were not allowed to freely organize political or cultural groups in the schools. Corporal punishment was meted out to those who objected to these repressive conditions. Disciplinary suspensions and expulsions were common.

To change these conditions a wave of Chicano high school blow outs (strikes) occurred all over the Southwest and in other places, like Chicago. The largest and most effective took place in 1968 in Los Angeles, where 15,000 Chicano students walked out of the barrio schools and triggered similar actions among students in some predominantly Black and several mostly white schools. A Chicano sit-in at the board of education brought to public attention the demands of Raza students for "Education, Not Contempt," "Education, Not Eradication," and posed the need for Chicano control of schools in the Chicano community. The actions of the high school students engendered support from college student groups as well as parent and community organizations.

Concessions have been granted as a result of these high school struggles, one of the most important being the repeal or easing of the prohibition against the teaching of regular classes in Spanish in the schools. But the Chicano people still face the problem of how to take control of the schools in the Chicano communities. Elements of control have been won in some school districts in South Texas, where student strikes have been combined with the formation of independent Chicano parties which have elected candidates to office.

Chicano college students also began to organize on the campuses for Chicano studies programs, open admissions, and community control of higher education—the Brown university. Chicano students played a leading role in the Third World Liberation Front strikes at San Franciso State College, the University of California at Berkeley, and elsewhere in 1968 and 1969. A Latin and Mexican-American studies department was won at Merritt College in Oakland and some form of Chicano studies was won at many other colleges.

A conference of Chicano students and educators in 1969 at Santa Barbara, California, issued *El Plan de Santa Bárbara* which "set out to formulate a Chicano plan for higher education."

Some elements of the concept of the Brown University are present in this document as summed up in the statement: "We do not come to work for the university, but to demand that the university work for our people."

No single Chicano student organization exists as a national or Southwest-wide group. UMAS (United Mexican-American Students) is strong in Colorado, MEChA (Movimiento Estudiantil Chicano de Aztlán—Chicano Student Movement of Aztlán) in California, MAYO (Mexican-American Youth Organization) in Texas. In the Midwest, Chicano students have in some cases united with Puerto Rican students in Latino groups such as the Latin American Student Organization in Chicago.

In many urban areas Chicano youth formed groups like the Brown Berets. These groups have played a role as organizers and monitors in high school strikes and in actions against police brutality. The Brown Berets vary from place to place, from being nonpolitical or antipolitical, to revolutionary nationalist, to ultraleft sectarian.

In those areas where independent Chicano political parties have been formed, student groups have often provided activists and leaders. This has been especially important in Texas, where MAYO-led student strikes helped lay the basis for the formation of La Raza Unida parties in South Texas.

La Raza and the War in Vietnam

The Vietnam War was escalated at a time of heightened nationalist consciousness among La Raza. Some Chicano leaders and organizations were among the most consistent and outspoken opponents of the war. As the antiwar movement grew, many activists became aware that masses of Chicanos could be mobilized in militant opposition to a war that was not in their interest. For one thing, Chicanos were being used as cannon fodder totally out of proportion to their numbers. For another, the Defense Department was giving a helping hand to the rich growers facing strikes by the farm workers by buying huge quantities of scab grapes and lettuce to feed to the U.S. troops in Vietnam. Increasing numbers of Chicanos asked the obvious question: "How can they tell us we are fighting for freedom and democracy 8,000 miles away, when we don't have freedom and democracy here at home?"

Chicano contingents in antiwar marches were organized in the late 1960s in places like Los Angeles, Denver, and San Francisco, and helped lay the basis for the unprecedented outpouring of La Raza for the National Chicano Moratorium to End the War in Vietnam on August 29, 1970, in East Los Angeles. Thirty thousand marched while additional tens of thousands lined the streets to cheer on the demonstrators.

The brutal police assault on the Chicano Moratorium rally and the East Los Angeles barrio resulted in the deaths of three Chicanos. This attack showed that the ruling class feared the prospect of mass mobilizations of Chicanos in the streets, especially when the idea of forming La Raza Unida parties was being popularized far and wide, including in Los Angeles. The greater Los Angeles area contains hundreds of thousands of Chicanos. Many live in unincorporated parts of Los Angeles County, the rest in an area gerrymandered to thwart the potential independent strength of the Chicano population as a single voting bloc.

The police attack brought about a sharp confrontation between an enraged community and the Los Angeles ruling class. First, the barrio erupted as many Chicanos gave vent to long pent-up rage at the conditions of life, the day-to-day police brutality, the profit-hungry merchants. Second, a sharp political struggle was waged to organize a mass street action to reassert the right to peaceably assemble for redress of grievances. Such an action was held on Mexican Independence Day. Ten thousand militant Chicanos marched despite the red-baiting campaign by city officials which was echoed by the reformists in the movement.

Further Chicano antiwar actions have since been held in widely scattered places, and sizable Chicano contingents have been organized for the subsequent coalition-called antiwar actions, most notably the huge April 24 march in San Francisco, where some 4,000 Chicanos and Latinos marched—the largest contingent of an oppressed nationality in that action.

Chicanas

Raza women have begun to discuss and act against their triple oppression as members of an oppressed nationality, as workers, and as females in a patriarchal bourgeois society. Most Chicanas are brought up in Catholic families, and thus have to cope with an especially reactionary morality which rationalizes the subordination of women in the family and in society, including strictures against the right of women to control their own bodies, the right to abortion and contraception.

The reactionary concepts about the role and rights of women perpetrated by capitalist society and religion are also promoted by some Chicano leaders in the name of *"La Familia de La Raza"* and machismo. The result is a denial of full opportunities for participation and leadership by Chicanas in the Chicano movement.

The May 1971 Mujeres Por La Raza (Women for La Raza) conference in Houston, attended by some 600 women, was an historic gathering. It showed the potential for mobilizing this half of La Raza as nationalist fighters and as feminists and points the way for women of other oppressed nationalities.

Immigration

The Immigration and Naturalization Service continues the policy of harassing and illegally deporting Chicanos and resident Mexicans to Mexico. This decades-old injustice has given rise to actions and organizations to expose these practices.

Catholics

Although more than half of the Catholics in the Southwest are Chicanos, the Catholic Church hierarchy has continuously insulted its Chicano membership by its racist practices and refusal to use its immense resources to support the Chicano movement. Groups have formed such as Católicos Por La Raza in Los Angeles, which has demonstrated at churches against the current state of affairs in Los Angeles County where, they say, property owned by the Catholic Church is valued in excess of $1 billion yet Chicano children "are praying to La Virgen de Guadalupe as they go to bed hungry."

The Development of Chicano Parties

The recent development of independent Chicano political parties that have contested in city, county, and state elections in several states in the Southwest grows out of the struggles outlined in the previous section and has profound implications for the Chicano people and for other oppressed nationalities, especially Afro-Americans.

For years Chicanos have voted in their majority, and in many cases overwhelmingly, for candidates of the Democratic Party. More than 95 percent of Chicanos voted for Democrats in 1956, 1958, 1960, 1962, and 1964. One of the most successful vote-hustling tools for John F. Kennedy in 1960 was the Viva Kennedy committees. Around the same time the Mexican-American Political Association (MAPA) and the Political Association of Spanish-speaking Organizations (PASO) were formed, which for the most part have faithfully delivered the Chicano vote to the Democrats.

One exception to this trend was the "third force" maneuver in 1966 in Texas, Arizona, and New Mexico to throw the Chicano vote to one major Republican candidate with the hope that this would make the Democrats more responsive to the aspirations of Chicanos. In Texas this maneuver resulted in the election of the Republican candidate, John Tower, to the U.S. Senate. A half-million Chicanos voted for Tower, and at the same time voted for the Democratic candidate for governor, John Connally, who also won. This resulted in the Johnson administration calling various moderate Chicano politicians to the White House to discuss holding a White House Conference on Mexican Americans. An earlier White House meeting with Black leaders had turned into an attack on the president so Johnson decided to hold the conference far away from Washington with militant Chicanos excluded. This caused such a furor among Chicano leaders that the conference was indefinitely postponed and never took place. But demands for action by the federal government continued to be pressed and the White House set up Cabinet hearings in El Paso in October of 1967. Invited were the more moderate leaders such as Chávez; excluded were Tijerina and others considered too militant.

Those excluded set up their own La Raza Unida conference attended by some 700 activists, including many who had been invited to the White House hearings. They held their own hearings and issued the *Plan de La Raza Unida*. This proclamation insisted that "the time of subjugation, exploitation, and abuse of human rights of La Raza in the United States is hereby ended forever." They drew up a list of demands directed at all levels of government, demands which were ignored by the

Johnson administration and the Democratic and Republican parties.

Subsequently, at the Democratic Party convention in 1968, Chicano Democrats complained that they were being ignored and considered walking out. Following the convention, California MAPA, which had always endorsed the Democratic Party nominees, voted not to endorse anyone for president. This was a factor in preventing a victory for Hubert Humphrey in California.

Though political associations like MAPA and PASO continue to endorse and get Raza votes for capitalist party candidates, they are pressured toward a more independent posture by the paucity of concessions emanating from these parties and by the insurgent Chicano movements, including the independent Chicano parties.

The formation of La Raza Unida parties signifies the beginnings of a break with this subordination to capitalist politics. These parties point the way toward registering in the electoral arena the strength, combativity, and independence of the mass struggles against the oppressive conditions of life forced on the Chicano people. They point to the need to generalize the various struggles of La Raza around education, the war, discrimination, and all the other issues into a unified, independent mass political struggle of Chicano people to take control of their own destiny. They show that meaningful victories can be achieved by combining electoral action with mass actions in the streets.

If these Raza Unida parties remain independent of the capitalist parties, including the national Democratic and Republican parties, and if they develop mass struggles centered on the needs of the Chicano people, they could be the first steps towards a mass independent Chicano political party.

Within the context of the deepening radicalization in the U.S. today, the development of a mass independent Chicano political party would shake up American politics. The strength of the Democratic Party comes from the support it receives from a combination of sizable oppressed groups—the trade unions, and the great majority of the Black and Chicano people. The coalition of these forces with the capitalist politicians of the Democratic Party is held together by the belief that this coalition can win elections and deliver reforms. The massive defection of Chicano voters would create an immediate crisis for all the elements in this coalition, not only in the Southwest, but nationally. Without the Chicano vote, the Democrats would be unable to carry whole sections of the Southwest and would be weakened in a number of midwestern states. The Democratic Party's growing incapacity to win nationally would break up this coalition, encouraging Black people and the labor movement to organize their own parties.

Old alignments would disintegrate and new ones form. A mass independent Chicano political party would therefore not only be the best way to promote and protect the welfare of the Chicano people, but would also create the possibility of forging alliances with other oppressed groups.

Meaningful improvements in the quality of life of the Chicano people under capitalism and ultimate liberation require a strategy of mass independent political action in all forms, and a militant leadership that can inspire and win the confidence of the masses. The forms this political action can take are many and varied. Thus far, the different components of the movement, such as student, labor, and antiwar struggles, have developed independently, each adopting organizational forms thought to be most suited to the demands being fought for, the milieu in which the struggle takes place, and the adversary being combatted. All these developed separately in the absence of an independent Chicano party enjoying the active support and adherence of the great mass of the Chicano people. If such a mass party had existed, the form and tempo of these struggles would undoubtedly have been different.

There are three interrelated aspects to building an independent Chicano party of mass action.

1. First is the organizing and carrying out of united-front mass actions. That is, actions around specific, well-defined issues organized in such a way that they are capable of drawing into motion the masses of La Raza. This requires an issue that is of immediate importance, formulated in a demand or demands easily understood, fought for by a leadership that wants to mobilize La Raza and is capable of forging the organizational means to that end, that is, a nonexclusive, democratic decision-making structure.

The building of such mass actions will help lay the basis for the development of an independent Chicano party. Where the nucleus of such a party exists, the building of united-front actions by that nucleus and other Raza forces will help it reach out to broader masses and at the same time project the independent Chicano party as a party capable of organizing the Chicano struggle on all fronts.

Aspects of the united-front approach existed in the organization for the National Chicano Moratorium Against the War, August 29, 1970. The issue was one of burning importance and immediacy. The central demand raised was basic, clear, and aimed squarely at the federal government: "Bring Our *Carnales* Home Now." The popular slogan *"Raza Si, Guerra No"* captured the nationalist spirit and dynamic of the Chicano Moratorium. The leadership of the Moratorium wanted a massive action and sought and welcomed the support of all, irrespective of their ideas on other issues. Many different groups and individuals were actively drawn into organizing the action.

Many local struggles in the high schools and colleges have likewise resulted in groups working together for mass actions which in some cases have involved considerable support and won their demands.

The mobilization of thousands of people in militant mass political action in the streets paves the way for independent political action in the electoral arena. This in turn can further spur on the independent mass street mobilizations. These two forms of political action should be seen as complementary and reinforcing, not as mutually exclusive or contradictory. In this way it will be made clear that an independent Chicano party must be a party of a new type, that is, a party of mass action.

2. The formulation of a mass action *program* of democratic and transitional demands will be fundamental to the development of a mass Chicano party.

3. Another important element in the construction of a mass Chicano party will be a nonexclusive, democratic structure open to all of La Raza who want to participate in the struggle. Internal democracy is important because it facilitates the fullest involvement of the masses of people, increases the likelihood that the party will faithfully reflect the aspirations of the most oppressed and exploited, and helps to ensure the selection and replenishment of leadership.

*   *   *

In the last two years a considerable number of leading Chicano activists have come to see the need to break with the capitalist parties and extend the independent thrust of the Chicano movement to the electoral arena through the formation of La Raza Unida parties and similar formations in Texas, Colorado, California, and Arizona. So far these attempts have resulted in a widespread popularization of the concept of independent electoral politics and have put on the defensive both the ultraleft abstentionists who reject any electoral activity on principle, and the opportunist Chicano Democratic and Republican politicians and those who support them.

The most outstanding results of these efforts have been the electoral victories in various city elections in South Texas where Chicanos constitute an overwhelming majority of the population.

In other areas, such as Colorado and California, good showings have been made by initiating nuclei of La Raza Unida parties. Though modest vote totals were achieved in the first attempts, the results were promising given the difficulties in launching any new political formation. Rather than causing a lapse into demoralization and inactivity, these modest successes have encouraged continued efforts. This is in sharp contrast to the earlier experience of the Black movement. Leaders of the Michigan Freedom Now Party in 1964 and the Lowndes County Freedom Organization in Alabama in 1966 and 1968 made promising first showings in electoral efforts, but became discouraged because they did not more quickly achieve a mass following, in the case of the FNP, or win an election victory, in the case of the LCFO. Both later returned to capitalist politics.

The advocates of independent Chicano parties have also avoided the error of merely proclaiming the formation of a nationwide or Southwest-wide political party, which would at this time be an artificial shell. While stating the need for a party based on all the Chicano people and making that their goal, these leaders have chosen to begin on a more realistic basis, on the state, county, and municipal level.

The Crystal City, Texas, Raza Unida Party grew out of militant student struggles in 1969. After the students and community came into conflict with the local government and won certain concessions, they saw the need to replace the racists and *vendidos* (Chicano sellouts) on the city council and school board with militant representatives of the Chicano community who had been tested in struggle. This led to the formation of La Raza Unida Party, which ran and won in the city elections and made changes beneficial to the Chicano community. At the same time

RUP supporters have continued to encourage further independent struggles such as participation in antiwar actions and the workers' fight for a democratic union in the main industrial plant in the area.

The meaningful changes made possible by combining mass action in the streets with independent electoral action included the firing of racist teachers, protecting high school student rights, outlawing corporal punishment by teachers, launching Chicano studies programs and bilingual education, and taking advantage of federal government monies they were entitled to but which were not utilized by the previous city government. Police policies were altered to the benefit of the Chicano community. La Raza Unida Party leaders also took immediate steps to substantially raise the wages of school and city workers and to encourage their unionization.

Steps were taken or projected to cope with the problem of involving the Chicano community in more direct, ongoing, and meaningful ways in policy decisions and implementation. One was the functioning of the Ciudadanos Unidos (United Citizens), originally set up as a parent support group during the school strikes in 1969, which later became a general adult leadership body. Another step was raising the idea of advisory councils, to be composed of democratically elected representatives from various constituencies—students, parents, teachers, and other school workers—to discuss and make decisions on key educational policy questions with the understanding that their decisions would be implemented by the city and school board officials elected on La Raza Unida Party's slate.

One of the principal achievements of the election victories in Crystal City is the psychological impact they have had, the inspiration and symbolic value of oppressed people wresting from their rulers some influence in public policy-making, some element of control over their lives and destiny.

While it is important to evaluate and publicize the Crystal City achievements, it is likewise essential to be aware of the limitations of this development. Crystal City is an isolated town of 10,000 people in a county of fewer than 15,000 in South Texas, 100 miles from San Antonio, the nearest large city. The economic mainstay of the county is agriculture and the small processing industries that exist are related to agriculture. Virtually all the land and agriculture-related industries in the county are owned by Anglos. Most of the commercial enterprises are Anglo-owned.

Moreover, many Crystal City Chicanos spend at least half of each year away from their homes as they fan out across the country in the spring to work in the fields, returning in late fall. Though this mobility helps spread the ideas and example of La Raza Unida Party to other areas it creates certain difficulties for local organizing.

Controlling the city hall and the school board in a town like Crystal City has strict limitations. There is only so much that can be changed through control of a city government, especially one which lacks financial resources. Beyond reach at the present time are the Anglo-owned businesses and the all-Anglo county government which wields considerably more power than the city because of its ability to tax the landowners in the county.

There are also leadership limitations. The central, militant leadership radicalized in the Chicano student movement is a small layer spread out in different cities in South Texas. Often the candidates chosen to run under the Raza Unida Party banner or other independent slates are less political, less radical than the former student leaders. Even among the most politically developed, there are different levels of understanding on key questions involving the capitalist parties, especially whether or not to support liberal Democrats like McGovern for president in 1972 on the national level or whether or not to have supported Yarborough for U.S. senator in Texas in 1970.

Programmatically these independent Texas formations aspire to Chicano control of South Texas, a majority-Chicano area of more than twenty-five counties. While they see the need to fight for attainable reforms that would improve their conditions, they don't necessarily pose the question of the need for more fundamental changes in society. The logic of fighting consistently for Chicano control of South Texas through all forms of independent mass political action points toward anticapitalist conclusions, but this is not widely understood among the activists and leaders of these independent developments.

Although La Raza Unida Party in Crystal City has mass support among Chicanos, the party itself is not yet a mass organization but rather more of an electoral instrument, set up to comply with Texas election laws. Those who register to vote RUP don't join a party with an organizational structure which can democratically involve the masses of La Raza. Instead, the decision-making groups that the political-minded activists belong to are Ciudadanos Unidos and MAYO.

The question of remaining independent of the capitalist parties and politicians is a decisive test facing the Raza Unida parties in Texas and elsewhere in the next period, especially as the 1972 presidential campaign approaches. We must expect that Democratic Party politicians, assisted by the labor bureaucracy, reformists in the Chicano movement, and the Communist Party, will be putting increasing pressure on the Raza Unida parties to support liberal Democrats and the national Democratic ticket, or perhaps some form of New Politics. Resisting this pressure will be essential to the continued development of the Raza Unida parties independent of the capitalist parties and based upon the Chicano people. The fact that some leaders of these parties have not unequivocally repudiated any support to the Democrats nationally, and have been attracted to Democratic presidential hopeful McGovern, highlights this danger. We will be participating in the political debates on this question, emphasizing the need for an independent mass Chicano political party.

Toward a Transitional Program for Chicano Liberation

One necessary step in the construction of a mass independent Chicano party is the elaboration of a program of democratic and transitional demands capable of mobilizing the masses of La Raza in struggle.

Attempts have been made to formulate such a program for Chicano liberation that would speak to the immediate day-to-day needs of the masses of La Raza—needs that American capitalism shows itself less and less able to meet in full—and at the same time point to the ultimate goal of Chicano liberation and self-determination.

Chicano control of the Chicano community is a central component of such a program. The demand that the Chicano community control through democratic means all institutions in the community arises from the experience of the Chicano people, who are exploited by Anglo business, brutalized by Anglo-controlled police forces, imprisoned unjustly by Anglo judges, drafted to fight by Anglo draft boards in a war that is not in their interest, miseducated and stripped of their language, history, and culture by the schools, excluded from or discriminated against in the trade unions, restricted from exercising constitutionally guaranteed rights of free speech, assembly, and redress of grievances.

Many demands have been put forward in the course of struggles in the last few years which constitute a starting point for developing a transitional program for Chicano liberation. *El Plan Espiritual de Aztlán* drawn up in 1969 at the Chicano Youth Liberation Conference in Denver was one contribution to the development of such a program. The 1970 platform of the Colorado Raza Unida Party and the initial programmatic documents of the Oakland-Berkeley Raza Unida Party were steps in the same direction.

The Delano Proclamation presented in 1966 by UFWOC, *El Plan de La Raza Unida, El Plan de Santa Bárbara, El Plan del Barrio* (issued during the Poor People's March on Washington) were additional programmatic manifestos and documents.

The goals of the high school student struggles must form part of such a program along with the goals of the farm workers' movement, Chicano workers in general, the college student organizations, the Bring Our *Carnales* Home movement, the prisoners, the women.

No full program for Chicano liberation has been developed, but some of the most important demands are clear. Some derive from the Transitional Program ("The Death Agony of Capitalism and the Tasks of the Fourth International") and can be directly applied to the Chicano struggle. Others were outlined in the transitional program for youth ("The Worldwide Youth Radicalization and the Tasks of the Fourth International"). Still others will be similar to demands in "A Transitional Program for Black Liberation." Some demands were raised in the programmatic section of "Toward a Mass Feminist Movement," which apply to Raza women.

Such demands as well as demands raised first in the Chicano movement will constitute the beginnings of a transitional program that can provide a guide for the organization and mobilization of the masses of La Raza. Such a program can point in the direction of mass anticapitalist mobilization, and lead toward the goal of Chicano liberation, and at the same time maximize the gains that can be won short of that goal. It will form a part of the general transitional program of the American socialist revolution.

The following is a contribution to the formulation of a transitional program for Chicano liberation.

1. The Right of Self-Determination

Since the Chicano people are oppressed as a nationality, they have the right to fully and unconditionally determine their own destiny, including the right to establish a separate state if they so decide collectively.

The most immediate and compelling struggles to determine the destiny of the Chicano people are those aiming at Chicano control of the Chicano community (or, as in a number of larger geographical areas where La Raza is a majority of the population, Chicano control of these regions, such as South Texas).

It is a democratic right of Chicanos to control all institutions in the Chicano community. These should be administered by democratically elected councils representing the masses of La Raza. These local councils should join with others on the state and national level on the basis of elected delegates subject to immediate recall.

2. Justice

Replace police occupation of the Chicano community with a police force composed of residents of the Chicano community and controlled by the Chicano community. Organize the community to defend itself.

La Raza has the right under the Constitution to trial by peers, and such trials should take place in Spanish if desired by the defendant. Release all Chicano prisoners who have not been tried by their peers.

Prisoners and ex-prisoners should retain citizenship rights of free speech, association, assembly, the right to hold and discuss ideas, the right to read and write what they choose with no censorship, and the right to vote. Regular conjugal visits should be provided for.

3. Education

The Chicano community shall have control of the education of La Raza through democratically elected councils. All of La Raza is entitled to free education through the university level with subsidies by the government to cover living expenses and books for those who otherwise wouldn't be able to go to school. From the earliest grades there should be instruction in the Spanish language as well as English. The true history and culture of the Chicano people must be taught to all.

In all educational institutions Chicano students must be allowed to exercise their constitutional rights without fear of disciplinary suspensions, expulsions, or corporal punishment. These include the right to hold and freely express ideas; the right to propagate these ideas through organizations, newspapers, leaflets, buttons; the right to use facilities of these public institutions to serve the needs of the Chicano people. End the tracking system.

All ties between the schools and the war machine must be severed. Student records must not be turned over to Selective Service. No military recruiters in the schools, no ROTC, no research for military purposes.

At both the high school and university level the student health services should include contraception and abortion facilities. Married or not, students with children shall not be expelled or suspended and shall be provided with free twenty-four-hour-a-day child care controlled by the students.

No cops on campus.

Teachers must abide by the will of the Chicano community. Racist teachers must be fired. Preferential training and hiring of Raza teachers. Teachers have the right to form unions, to bargain collectively, and to strike.

4. Chicano Workers

All Chicano workers, including farm workers, shall have the right to organize unions and to strike for higher wages and better working conditions. Farm workers shall be covered by minimum wage and workmen's compensation legislation. End all residency requirements so that migrant laborers qualify for all national, state, and local welfare and other benefits.

Growers and other bosses shall be prevented from strikebreaking practices by the establishment of union-controlled hiring halls. For full union democracy, including the right to organize Chicano caucuses to fight against racist union officials and practices.

For a sliding scale of wages and hours so that all who want to work can do so and so that inflation doesn't wipe out wage gains. An escalator clause in all union contracts so that wages automatically rise with the cost of living. A shorter workweek with no loss in pay to spread the available work so that there will be jobs for all.

Preferential hiring and training of Chicanos to make up for

past and present discriminatory hiring practices. No federal government money to construction projects where Chicanos are not hired at least in proportion to the population.

5. *Raza Women*

Chicanas have the right as women to control their lives and destinies. End all discrimination against Chicanas. Equal pay for equal work, equal job and educational opportunities; free twenty-four-hour child care controlled by the parents and community; repeal all laws restricting the right to abortion; free abortion on demand; no forced sterilization; the right to contraceptive devices and information.

6. *Election Laws*

Repeal all state election laws that restrict the participation of independent Chicano candidates and parties in local, state, and federal elections, including prohibitive registration or signature requirements, distribution requirements, loyalty oaths, filing fees, and gerrymandering of election districts to the detriment of La Raza.

For the full franchise at eighteen years old: the right to vote in all elections and the right of *any* qualified voter to run for and hold any public office. Print official election material, including ballots, in English and Spanish.

7. *Against Mass-Media Stereotypes*

The FCC shall revoke the licenses of radio and television stations that use racist stereotypes to portray Chicanos in advertising and programming. No racist stereotypes in newspapers, textbooks, and other forms of mass communication.

8. *Foreign Policy*

End the drafting of Chicano youth to fight in imperialist wars. End the war in Southeast Asia and bring the *carnales* home now. Bring all U.S. troops home from Southeast Asia now. Support the constitutional rights of Chicanos in the armed forces to organize and to express political views and cultural pride.

Support the national liberation struggles of oppressed peoples. End U.S. government intervention in Latin America.

9. *Land*

Land to those who work it. Nationalize the "factory farms" under farm workers' control.

10. *Formation of a Chicano Political Party*

The indispensable instrument for organizing and carrying on effective struggle for such demands, achieving Chicano control of the Chicano community, and moving forward to Chicano liberation is a mass independent Chicano political party.

Tasks of the SWP

In aiding the development of an independent mass Chicano movement, the Socialist Workers Party must help popularize the ideas of and help in other ways to build the Chicano parties, the Chicano antiwar movement, the high school and college struggles, and other important actions, including the farm workers' and boycott movements, the struggles of Raza women, the developing movement of Chicano prisoners, and the defense of victims of political frame-ups. In this work we advance our program and perspective for Chicano liberation.

In the coming debates on the 1972 elections, we can play an important role in fighting for the maintenance of an independent perspective, arguing against any support to the capitalist parties, either direct support to the Democrats or Republicans, or through New Politics tickets or parties.

Such tasks are the responsibility of the entire party and must not fall solely to Chicano and Latino members. Due to our limited forces a premium is placed on extensive use of the socialist press for getting out our ideas—the *Militant,* the *International Socialist Review,* and Pathfinder Press literature—as well as SWP election campaigns and our weekly forums.

The *Militant* above all enables us to regularly speak to thousands of people, including many activists in the Chicano movement, and to extend our political influence beyond our numbers. Sales of individual copies and subscriptions to the *Militant* to Chicano activists must be seen as part of our regular sales efforts.

These vehicles enable us to present news and analysis of the Chicano movement and other initiatives of the oppressed and exploited and counterpose our full program for social change in polemics against the reformists and ultralefts.

Chicano and Latino members should help build Chicano student, antiwar, and feminist groups, and La Raza Unida Party formations. Where it is not possible to participate actively in the Chicano movement our strength in the student, antiwar, and women's liberation movements can be utilized to make contact with and help the independent development of La Raza, and at the same time encourage the Chicano movement to unite in broadly based mass-action coalitions. We should be alert to opportunities to support struggles of Chicano workers.

Unfortunately, red-baiting has marred certain Chicano struggles. We should expose red-baiting for what it is—an attempt to divide the Chicano movement and to weaken its more militant wing. When directed specifically against us, it is in reality aimed at all those, including ourselves, who are consistent fighters for the political independence of the Chicano movement.

In addition to supporting Chicano antiwar actions we must help build Raza antiwar contingents such as were organized for the April 24 antiwar marches. Chicana contingents in mass women's demonstrations, such as the abortion law repeal actions, should also be built.

Part of the preparation for meaningful participation in the Chicano movement is learning from that movement. In this connection it is important to read Chicano newspapers and magazines and hold educationals on the history and current stage of the struggle of the Chicano people. To equip our members to understand and help provide leadership for the Chicano movement they must study the Marxist analysis of the national question, the theory of the permanent revolution, the history of struggles of other oppressed nationalities in this country, and the history of the working class movement.

One of the tasks of the coming American revolution will be carrying through to completion the struggle of the Chicano people for self-determination, which cannot be won under capitalism; the full liberation of Chicanos, both as part of the working class and as a nationality, can be achieved only through a victorious socialist revolution.

An absolutely essential prerequisite for the success of the coming American revolution is the construction of a mass revolutionary socialist party on the Leninist model. The construction of such a party is the central objective of the SWP.

The mass revolutionary socialist party we seek to build must be multinational as well as proletarian in composition, uniting revolutionary Marxists from the different nationalities in this country into a single centralized combat party. At the present stage of building such a party, the recruitment and training of cadres is our foremost task. More and more Chicano activists will join the SWP as they come to see the need for a socialist revolution and for a Leninist party to lead that revolution to victory, a party with a correct program on all aspects of the anticapitalist struggle, that unconditionally supports the fight of the Chicano people for self-determination, fights alongside them for their full liberation, and fights for the full liberation of all humanity.

Chicano Liberation Report to the 1971 SWP Convention

This report was given by Antonio Camejo to the August 1971 SWP convention.

In his discussion of nationalities in *The History of the Russian Revolution* Leon Trotsky pointed out that it was only after the February 1917 revolution that several of the most oppressed nationalities in tsarist Russia began formulating their aspirations for self-determination. Some others were aroused only after the socialist revolution of October that year. The heightening of the class struggle in Russia rapidly precipitated the hopes and demands of even the smallest oppressed national groupings.

We are now witnessing a comparable phenomenon *prior* to the socialist revolution in the United States because of the peculiar development of U.S. capitalism and also in response to the heightening of the class struggle on a world scale, especially the colonial revolution. The profound Black nationalist radicalization and the entrance of the Chicano people onto the political stage of the current radicalization are dramatic verifications of the depth of this radicalization and give us further clues to the dynamic of the coming American revolution.

In the 1969 party discussion George Breitman pointed out that, if the upsurge in the class struggle had continued after the Second World War, and if the working class had been able to deepen the radicalization of the 1930s, to form a mass revolutionary party and start on the road to power, then the subsequent radicalization of oppressed nationalities would have proceeded along different lines. But that potential upsurge was thwarted and a general retreat and decline of the labor movement set in. This turn of events not only affected subsequent developments but has influenced the manner in which social struggle has begun to manifest itself in the present radicalization.

Chicanos, suffering a dual oppression—that is, oppressed because of their race, culture, and language, and for the most part exploited as workers—looked hopefully to the rise of the Congress of Industrial Organizations (CIO) and participated in its formation and struggles. With the decline in militancy of the class as a whole, neither Blacks nor Chicanos were prepared to await a renewed upsurge of the labor movement before beginning to deal with their special problems as oppressed nationalities. They began radicalizing in their own ways, conditioned by this turn of events in the class struggle as a whole, by their own history and conditions of life, and by international factors. The recent upsurge of Chicano nationalism flows out of this particular conjuncture and bears its indelible stamp.

At a National Committee plenum in February 1970, Jack Barnes pointed out how the rise of nationalist struggles in the 1960s was characterized by the independence, self-organization, self-confidence, and self-mobilization that occurred prior to alliances with other major forces, and outside the control of the trade union bureaucracy or the Communist Party.

This independent thrust of the rise of Chicano nationalism is central to an understanding not only of the Chicano struggle but of the present radicalization as a whole. We can confidently say that both Black and Chicano nationalism are here to stay, not only until the socialist revolution but also after the American working class comes to power. The existence of mass nationalist organizations of La Raza will play an important role, not only in the making of the socialist revolution, but in facilitating the resolution of the national question after the overthrow of capitalist rule.

From the experiences of the Russian and Cuban revolutions in particular, we can predict that nationalist consciousness will grow with the heightening of the class struggle, not disappear before or with it. As Trotsky observed in his writings between 1939 and 1940, the national struggle is itself one of the most complex, yet extremely important, forms of the class struggle.

The nationalist consciousness of La Raza flows from the pattern of oppression which is a fact of daily life. The resolution, "The Struggle for Chicano Liberation," points out: "Except for Native Americans, Chicanos suffer the highest unemployment, the lowest per capita income, the worst education, the highest functional illiteracy rate, the highest death rate, occupy the most dilapidated and overcrowded housing, and have less political representation in local, state, or national government than any nationality in the population of the Southwest and perhaps in the nation."

Another aspect of this pattern of oppression is the suppression of the Spanish language. Through their attempt to obliterate the Spanish language, the ruling class hoped to strip Mexicanos of their history, culture, and identity in the same manner as the slave masters stripped the African slaves of their languages and original identities. So English-speaking Canada has attempted to undermine the French language of the Québécois.

Although the ruling class never fully succeeded in this regard, they have left their mark upon the generations of linguistically handicapped Chicanos who have had their native tongue cut out, either partially or completely, and are left without a full proficiency in English because of racist educational institutions. It is clear that the suppression of the Spanish language remains a critical ingredient in the oppression of Chicanos.

As outlined in the article, "The Forging of an Oppressed Nationality" [included in this book], the expansion of the southern slavocracy and northeastern capitalism led to the forging of the Mexican inhabitants of the conquered provinces of northern Mexico into a distinct oppressed nationality. The Mexican frontier settlements had already developed a certain autonomy from the central administration in Mexico City, as well as an independent outlook, well before the Anglo invasion. The conquest of that area, one-half the national territory of Mexico, definitively put an end to the direçt influence by Mexico's ruling class over the Mexican people in that territory.

Capitalist property relations violently displaced all forms of precapitalist and semifeudal means of exploitation in California, and, after the Civil War, throughout the Southwest. Mexican landowners, independent miners, and traders were either directly expropriated or driven into the ranks of the working class by the English-speaking foreigners. The Mexican people of the Southwest were violently coerced into the position of an oppressed nationality. Then the new waves of immigrants from Mexico during the first half of this century were forced into this mold of national oppression by the capitalist ruling class and its institutions.

Increased urbanization, the difference in class relationships, and other factors have all tended to shape Chicanos into a nationality which is similar to, but distinct from, that of Mexico. While Chicanos clearly do not fit into the Anglo cultural norms, neither do they fit into those of Mexico. La Raza in the Southwest has a culture distinct from that of Mexico, and in addition, speaks both a dialect of Spanish and a language not spoken in Mexico—English. The dynamic of Chicano nationalism is one of self-determination as a unique oppressed nationality. Its direction is not for a reunification with bourgeois Mexico.

The Development of Chicano Parties

Although the nationalist aspirations of the Chicano people have recently taken many different forms, such as the farm workers' struggles, the land-grant movement, the high school blowouts, campus struggles, and the Chicano antiwar moratoriums, the thrust has been the same: an attempt by La Raza to protect itself against the evils of U.S. capitalism and to determine its own destiny, to take control of the institutions within the Chicano communities which directly affect the lives, labor, and well-being of Chicanos.

One of the most important advances in the struggle for self-determination has been the formation of La Raza Unida parties, particularly the Raza Unida Party in southwestern Texas, which has succeeded for the first time in scoring several electoral victories and gaining local governmental positions in Crystal City. These initial victories by an independent Chicano political party have set an example for all oppressed national minorities in this country, as well as for the labor movement.

They surely have had a great impact on the Chicano struggle as a whole. The capitalist ruling class has not been slow in recognizing the serious threat which this development could pose if picked up by the masses of Chicanos. In a speech in the spring of 1971 before the California Democratic Council, Senator George McGovern, an announced presidential candidate, warned that the

Democratic Party had better start giving Chicanos more voice in the party and more representation in government.

He pointed out: "This is not simply an altruistic position for the Democratic Party to take. It is necessary for the survival of the Democratic Party as the party of all the people." McGovern went on to say: "If the Democratic Party does not take positive steps to include America's minorities *in*—and not just with rhetoric but a full share of power—the day will surely come when those minorities will leave the Democratic Party *out* in the political cold.

"You can't play games with people any more. You either give them what they deserve or they will give you what you deserve."

One of the things troubling not only McGovern but Nixon is a recent study released by the League of United Latin American Citizens and the Mexican-American Bar Association. This study revealed that, based on the 1960 and 1968 presidential election patterns, a shift of even 6 percent in the Chicano vote in California, Texas, Illinois, and New Mexico could determine the outcome of the 1972 presidential elections.

It is no surprise then that we find the following in the August 6, 1971, *New York Times:* "Henry M. Ramirez, a one-time migrant worker in California, was named by President Nixon yesterday as chairman of the Cabinet Committee on Opportunities for Spanish-Speaking Peoples. He is the first Hispanic-American to serve on the President's staff." So you see, the Socialist Workers Party is not the only one preparing for 1972. We are not the only ones who see the significance of the initial steps toward building an independent Chicano party.

Our concept of an independent Chicano political party is that it will be a mass party that can mobilize Chicanos in action in the streets, as well as confront the ruling class in the electoral arena. The need for such a party flows directly out of the Chicano struggle itself and its present level of consciousness.

The development and experience of the Lowndes County Freedom Organization in Alabama, the Freedom Now Party in Michigan, and the Black Panther Party, have helped to enrich our understanding of what kind of party it must be, the difficulties to be encountered and the errors to be avoided. They have helped to further refine our concept of independent political action by an oppressed nationality. The lessons we have drawn from the Black struggle have enabled us to play an important role in propagandizing for an independent Chicano party.

Although no such mass independent Chicano party has yet developed, the experiences of the initiating nuclei of such parties in Texas, Colorado, and northern California have helped to deepen the general understanding of the importance of breaking with the capitalist parties, popularizing La Raza Unida Party among broad layers of the Chicano community.

The concrete changes that the Crystal City Raza Unida Party has been able to make have improved the schools of Crystal City and somewhat reduced the grosser forms of oppression suffered by La Raza. These modest gains for the better are dismissed by purist sectarians as "Brown sewer socialism." But I should point out that at least one-third of the Chicanos in Crystal City don't even have sewers or running water.

The victories have also shown the distinct limitations of organizing on only a local level, as well as the fact that political office is not state power—it does not change the basic economic relationship of land ownership or the exploitation of Chicano workers.

In Colorado the RUP has been based primarily on the resources and leadership of the Crusade for Justice, which is centered in Denver. While the RUP intervened in the lettuce strike in the San Juan and San Luis valleys of Colorado in 1970, giving support to the farm workers, pressure from the AFL-CIO bureaucrats forced the leader of that strike into withdrawing as a Raza Unida candidate. A modest but encouraging vote was received by the Colorado RUP last November, but this effort was not matched in last spring's Denver city elections.

The developments in northern California, with energetic campaigns by several candidates, have shown the potential for organizing a statewide party there.

Key to the building of mass independent Raza Unida parties is the development and implementation of a program of democratic and transitional demands which can mobilize the Chicano community in mass action against the specific conditions of their oppression.

What Is Our Program?

The basic components of a program for Chicano liberation flow from the nature of the oppression suffered by La Raza. Since Chicanos are not only exploited as workers but are also oppressed as a nationality, they have the right to fully and unconditionally determine their own destiny, including the right to establish a separate state if they so decide collectively. The demand for Chicano control of the Chicano community is a concretization of this right of self-determination. It is a basic democratic right that Chicanos control all the institutions within the Chicano community. The fight around control of specific institutions in the Chicano community, such as the schools, can serve to mobilize broad layers of the community and raise their consciousness about the nature of their oppression.

Self-determination for oppressed nationalities is one of the uncompleted democratic tasks of the American bourgeois revolutions, a task which can now only be carried out through the socialist revolution. The overwhelmingly proletarian composition of the Chicano nationality requires that a program for Chicano liberation include a series of demands aimed at mobilizing Chicano workers against capitalist exploitation. It is the combining of the national-democratic tasks left over from the epoch of the bourgeois revolution with the proletarian tasks of the socialist revolution which gives the Chicano struggle its profoundly revolutionary dynamic. It is the Chicano working masses who will be in the forefront of the Chicano liberation struggle, as well as in the vanguard of the working class struggle as a whole in the coming American revolution.

The basis for a transitional program for Chicano liberation as developed in the resolution does not come from a rewording of "A Transitional Program for Black Liberation." It encompasses many demands which have been raised over the past several years in the course of the Chicano struggle itself. *El Plan Espiritual de Aztlán, El Plan de Delano, El Plan de la Raza Unida, El Plan del Barrio,* and *El Plan de Santa Bárbara* are some contributions toward formulating such a program. This document attempts to apply the method and strategy of the Transitional Program, "The Death Agony of Capitalism and the Tasks of the Fourth International." It incorporates aspects of the programmatic section of "Toward a Mass Feminist Movement," as well as "A Transitional Program for Black Liberation." Such a program, based on the objective needs as well as the present consciousness of La Raza, can point in the direction of mass anticapitalist mobilization, and lead toward the goal of Chicano liberation, while at the same time maximizing the gains that can be won short of that goal.

Political Opponents in the Chicano Movement

Among the incorrect perspectives for the Chicano movement is that of the liberals. They make the error of believing that the problems of Chicanos can be solved under capitalism. The axis of their strategy is characterized by their attempt to look to one or another section of the ruling class to grant token concessions, in particular the liberal wing of the Democratic Party. An example of this outlook is a Mexican-American Political Association (MAPA) brochure which states: "We have contended since our inception that, with a sound political instrument at our command we would again reenter the political arena and again become a part of the total economic and political life of our country."

Founded by Chicano Democrats, MAPA has mobilized the Chicano vote for the Democratic Party in almost every election since 1960. Other Chicano organizations such as PASO (Political Association of Spanish-speaking Organizations), the GI Forum, the League of United Latin American Citizens (LULAC), and the Congress of Mexican-American Unity (CMAU) have a similar orientation.

The most serious of our political opponents within the Chicano movement is the Stalinist Communist Party. Together with the liberals in the Chicano community, they have been instrumental in keeping La Raza tied to capitalist politics. Starting with their "popular front" period in the 1930s, they used their influence in the Chicano community and particularly among Chicano trade unionists to tie Chicanos to the Democratic Party through the Roosevelt campaign in 1936. During the Second World War they urged Chicanos to enlist in the armed forces to fight in what they characterized as a "war for democracy." In the July 1949 issue of *Political Affairs,* the theoretical journal of CPUSA, under a section entitled "The Mexican People and the War," they state, ". . . Mexicans have continued to contribute to the nation's progress and made *an outstanding contribution* to the *war effort"* (emphasis added).

After supporting the imperialist war the Stalinists mobilized the Chicano people to support the Progressive Party campaign of capitalist politician Henry Wallace. They played a key role in an organization called Amigos de Wallace, which they used to hustle the Chicano vote. In the same issue of *Political Affairs* the CP evaluated the 1948 Wallace campaign as representing for the

Chicano people ". . . the highest stage of political development and activity since the unemployed struggles of the 30's."

The present goal of the Communist Party for the creation of what they call a "New People's Party" is no different from the class-collaborationist Progressive Party of 1948. In the "New Program of the Communist Party, U.S.A.," adopted by their nineteenth National Convention in 1969, they state the following: "We are for maximum political struggle, for independent positions and forms, within the two-party vise. But the historical direction we see in this struggle, the desired goal, is creation of a new people's party." Their concept of a procapitalist third party is directly counterposed to an independent Chicano political party, which is a nationalist formation independent of the capitalist class. Until the forces are assembled for such a third capitalist party, the CP contends that the electoral expression of the Chicano movement ". . . necessarily continues mainly within the Democratic Party, because of the overwhelming participation in the Mexican community in that particular organization" (*Viva La Raza, A Communist View on Chicano Liberation*). And they want to keep it there!

The Communist Party's role has been to subordinate the Chicano struggle to the foreign policy needs of the Soviet bureaucracy. Thus during the "third period" (1928-35) ushered in by Stalin, they built "red" trade unions among Chicano farm workers. These led to numerous victimizations of workers, including deportations; then the CP abandoned those unions when the Kremlin changed its line to that of the popular front. While in 1932 they denounced Roosevelt as a fascist and an imperialist, in 1936 they were urging everyone to defeat Landon, the Republican candidate, "at all costs," thus signaling to those they influenced to vote for FDR in preference to the CP candidate.

Although the CP claims to be for the right of self-determination for the Chicano people, in reality they view this demand as a tactic, not a principle. In a report to a recent National Committee meeting of the Communist Party, their reporter said the following: "We must put forth a slogan of self-determination of destiny for the Mexican (*sic*) movement, *to stay with the tempo and the mood of that movement today*" (emphasis added). "The character of the self-determination, as Lenin ably pointed out, is determined by the historical conditions when socialism is established." Meaning, of course, that they reserve the right to drop the slogan if the Chicano movement develops in a manner that cuts across their class-collaborationist schemes or the needs of the Soviet bureaucracy. On the theoretical as well as the practical level the Stalinists oppose the independent thrust of Chicano nationalism.

One way the CP covers its support to the Democratic Party in California is to blast Los Angeles mayor Sam Yorty while supporting other Democrats such as Senator John Tunney and Congressman Ed Roybal. Thus *La Marcha de la Reconquista,* in which the CP has significant influence, has issued leaflets calling for Chicanos to register in La Raza Unida Party and at the same time warning that the central need is to prevent Yorty from being the Democratic Party nominee for president.

Since the upheaval on August 29, 1970, in East L.A., some leaders of the Chicano Moratorium Committee who were influenced by the CP have retreated from building mass actions against the war. The Communist Party remains our main opponent within the Chicano movement and an obstacle to building a mass independent Chicano political party.

Other incorrect strategies are put forward by the ultraleftists and by the antinationalist sectarians. The militancy and combativeness among barrio youth was revealed in the aftermath of the police attack on the Chicano Moratorium in East L.A. This same combativity, an expression of deepening nationalist sentiment, was again expressed in the upheaval in Albuquerque this summer, which resulted from an incident involving police brutality. The rebellion in Albuquerque was due to smoldering frustrations in the barrio similar to the conditions which touched off the Black rebellions in 1965 and 1967. But this is quite different from the conscious adventuristic strategy of groups such as the Brown Berets in a number of areas, the Chicano Revolutionary Party (now the Raza Revolutionary Party), and the sectarian socialist tendencies such as the Workers League, the Progressive Labor Party, and the Spartacist League.

Groups such as the Brown Berets, in most places, and the Raza Revolutionary Party attempt to substitute a small vanguard for the mass mobilization of the Chicano community. They reject the possibility of organizing and mobilizing the Chicano community and instead project "armed struggle" by small groups. The Raza Revolutionary Party (RRP) in East Oakland, patterned after the Black Panther Party, tried to do the Panthers one better with their slogan, "Dare to Struggle, Dare to Win, Shoot to Kill." They refused to support the 1971 Raza Unida Party election campaign in East Oakland. Although most of these youth have been students at Merritt College at one time or another, they belittle Chicano students and the concept of the Brown university. To a mass struggle perspective that includes using the bourgeois educational institutions as organizing centers to reach out to and mobilize the Chicano community around immediate, democratic, and transitional demands, the RRP counterposes a "serve the people" counterinstitutionalism. Their rhetoric of "being on the streets where the people are" and "relating to the people where they are at" amounts to nothing more than social workerism and doing nothing to involve the masses in struggle around demands aimed at the government. By trying to play at having state power and "feeding the masses" (usually about thirty children) they take the capitalist government off the hook.

The Brown Berets in East L.A., who are composed predominantly of working class barrio youth, use a lot of ultraleft Maoist rhetoric. But they became totally paralyzed when a real mass upheaval and confrontation with the police took place in the Chicano community after the Chicano Moratorium. Their response was to go underground. They had no idea of how to respond effectively to the ruling class attack.

The development of mass actions such as the Chicano Moratorium and the establishment of Raza Unida parties have helped to cut across ultraleftism and expose the inadequacy and incorrectness of this line in some cases.

Among the antinationalist sectarians is the Healyite Workers League. Besides their distortions of what Lenin and Trotsky had to say on the national question they have made some odd contributions to the general theoretical impoverishment of ultraleft sectarians. In their pamphlet *Black Nationalism and Marxist Theory,* the Workers League makes the following observation: "It is precisely the fact that the bourgeois revolution has long been completed in Belgium, England, Canada, and the United States which makes the current nationalist and seminationalist movements in these countries so completely reactionary and the demand for the right to self-determination absolutely out of place." The fact is, however, that for La Raza, for Black people, and for other oppressed minorities, many elementary bourgeois democratic rights have yet to be granted under U.S. capitalism. It has been the inability of U.S. capitalism to assimilate these peoples with full rights into Anglo-American society politically, economically, and culturally, that has left certain tasks of the two bourgeois revolutions in this country unfinished. That and that alone is what gives the coming socialist revolution its combined character. If the democratic tasks of the bourgeois revolution have been completed, then, you see, there is no national question. That simplifies the problem exceedingly. It is only a matter of workers in general overthrowing capitalism. That is why the Workers League can say with a straight face that the nationalist demand for Black control of the Black community ". . . only proposes that the blacks separate themselves from the whites and administer their own oppression."

They go on to say, "Such a 'reform' changes nothing essential to capitalist survival and in fact contributes to that survival by isolating the black workers from the rest of the working class and bringing them closer to the bourgeoisie." They miss the small fact that it's the ruling class that has isolated Black and Chicano workers from the rest of the working class, and that the self-organization of the oppressed is an essential step toward their liberation, as well as toward real alliances with other sections of the working class.

Like the Communist Party, the Progressive Labor Party projects a fight against an abstract conception of racism and in practice sees the members of oppressed nationalities solely as workers. PLP [which was then Maoist] was at the height of its influence in the Chicano movement during the Third World Liberation Front strike at San Francisco State College in 1968 and 1969. They have since sharply declined and are now the most despised of the antinationalist sectarians within the Chicano movement.

What the logic of seeing only the class aspect of the oppression of national minorities leads to is reflected in the Spartacist League, which views the Raza Unida Party as petty bourgeois. This is what they say: "Because the leadership of La Raza Unida focus their efforts almost exclusively on winning city council elections in various towns, and because the program of La Raza Unida is vague and 'class independent,' while at the same time profoundly reformist—we characterize it as a petty-bourgeois party and our attitude is one of opposition and sharp criticism." They hasten to add, however: "Our tactical approach is somewhat more friendly as we seek to break the ranks and the best of the leadership of La Raza Unida away from classless third partyism, and win them to the fight for a workers party." And for Chicano nationalists who feel left in the lurch they add, "Chicanos can form the backbone of the Texas chapter of a nationwide labor party."

The inability to comprehend the oppression of La Raza on the basis of race, language, and culture, as well as their superexploitation as part of the working class—the dual character of their oppression—is what characterizes all of the reformists as well as the ultraleftists and sectarians. This is their common error. Under pressure from the ruling class all have buckled on the fundamental question of the right of oppressed national minorities to determine their own destiny. This is an antisocialist and antidemocratic attitude.

Yet another current within the Chicano movement is composed of revolutionary nationalists. They are distinguished from the liberals, reformists, ultraleftists, and sectarians by their general understanding of, and support for, what is to one degree or another an independent mass-action perspective. They best express the independent thrust of Chicano nationalism, its uncompromising attitude toward all forms of oppression, and its logic toward an alliance with a revitalized labor movement.

Many people have incorrectly referred to the liberals as cultural nationalists to distinguish them from the revolutionary nationalists. But cultural nationalism is the one thing they have in common. Both support the need to study Chicano history and to build pride in their Indian and Mexican heritage and culture. What separates them is the fact that the liberals and reformists think Chicano oppression can be ended under capitalism, while the revolutionary nationalists are aiming more and more for a complete break from the system.

The term *cultural nationalists* has been used in a derogatory way by the Black Panther Party in their *retreat* from Black nationalism. Around the same time that they began to popularize that term they dropped the nationalist slogan "Black Power to Black People," and began using the slogan "Power to the People." This latter slogan has been encouraged by the CP as well because it has a deceptively dual character. It both facilitates the blurring of class lines and is antinationalist in spirit.

We support the fight of the Chicano people to reassert their language, their music, their folklore, and other aspects of their culture. This is necessary and progressive. What we point out is that this alone cannot bring about liberation, and that an unrestricted rebirth of the cultural inheritance of the Southwest will only come about as the result of a political and social struggle for complete self-determination.

Revolutionary nationalists such as Corky Gonzáles, José Angel Gutiérrez, and others, have so far generally avoided the traps of adventurism by trying to reach out and mobilize the Chicano community. Gonzáles, in particular, has supported and helped to build mass actions against the war, as well as the Denver high school blowouts. Since his break with the Democratic Party he has maintained an independent nationalist organization—the Crusade for Justice—with support among broad layers of the Chicano community.

Many revolutionary nationalists, however, have no clear, thought-out perspective of how liberation will be won. Thus they are subject to pressure from the liberals and reformists, leading them sometimes to red-bait socialists in the movement and at other times to use ultraleft rhetoric and engage in ultraleft actions. While generally sympathetic to our socialist views, they have not yet fully come to the conclusion that only socialism can provide the solution to the national oppression and class exploitation of the Chicano people. This will become clearer as the struggle unfolds, and we can expect to win many of these militant activists to the banner of revolutionary socialism.

Our Critics in the SWP

The "For a Proletarian Orientation" minority tendency (FAPO) in the SWP makes many of the same mistakes as our ultraleft sectarian opponents.* In the three line-resolutions presented as the basis for their tendency and for reorienting the party, their analysis of the present nationalist movements, and particularly

---

*The "For a Proletarian Orientation" tendency in the SWP was formed in 1971. It argued that the SWP had abandoned its orientation to the working class and that massive colonization of certain industries was immediately necessary. It eventually fragmented, and many of its leaders left the SWP.

of the Chicano movement, is both inadequate and incorrect. They give absolutely no analysis of the two most important developments in the nationalist movement over the past two years, namely, the Raza Unida parties and the Chicano antiwar movement, particularly the Chicano Moratorium of August 29, 1970.

In their first document, "For a Proletarian Orientation," they quote Comrade Frank Lovell to this effect: "The labor party movement may well be sparked by the successful efforts of the Raza Unida Party or the organization of an independent all-Black mass party." They then add in ridicule, "The workers, don't you see, will automatically follow the examples of Blacks and Chicanos." But in their second document, entitled "The Meaning of a Proletarian Orientation," they explain the meaning of this supposedly incorrect view of Lovell's by, surprisingly enough, agreeing with him. They state: "In addition, of course, successful Black and Raza Unida parties *must* be based on Black and Chicano workers. The lessons will not go unnoticed by the white working class, either." That is the extent of their reference to this major development (i.e., the Raza Unida parties).

In all three of their documents they present a vague conception of community struggles, which they limit to struggles around what they define as class demands. In *none* of the documents do they raise the question of Chicano control of the Chicano community, either for or against. Do they perhaps feel that this demand can only mean that the Chicano community will come under the control of the Chicano bourgeoisie? Although they don't state that, such is the logic of their position.

If we were to base our orientation toward the Raza Unida parties on the basis of what is contained in the three tendency documents all we would have to go on is that the Raza Unida Party must be based on workers. Their failure even to mention the Chicano Moratorium and its impact on the Chicano community shows either ignorance of what is happening there or a complete lack of understanding of how to even begin an analysis. Invariably when they mention Chicanos it's only as an *adjective* preceding the *noun* worker. This tells a lot about their real position.

This one-sided view of the oppression of La Raza leans dangerously close to the antinationalist position of the Workers League or PLP, in spite of occasional FAPO statements that they support the right of self-determination. One can only have grave doubts about this when they agree that the revolution will have a combined character and then refer only to *half* of the combination, and incorrectly at that.

Another document, "Third World Work and a Proletarian Orientation," has been presented to the party as a counterresolution to "The Struggle for Chicano Liberation." This document does not offer a viable alternative to the party's program and in fact contains serious shortcomings, erroneous conceptions of how the nationalist radicalization of Chicanos has taken place, and incorrect views on the question of party-building and the party's past activities within the Chicano movement.

One of the strangest things about the "Third World Work" counterresolution is that it makes no mention *whatsoever* of the resolution which it counters. It has no analysis of where our resolution goes wrong, what its shortcomings are and why it must be rejected. It presents no program for intervening in the Chicano struggle other than the abstract call for going to the community and the working class, as was made in the three Proletarian Orientation tendency documents. They outlined no specific tasks whatsoever for the party to carry out in this sector in the coming period.

Although they mention community control, it is only in relation to Chicano *workers,* both men and women, and with no analysis of the nationalist dynamic of the struggle for Chicano control of the Chicano community. It makes no sense to talk about being in favor of self-determination without giving an analysis of the concretization of that right in the democratic demand for Chicano control of the Chicano community.

For all their talk about doing Chicana work they don't even mention the historic Chicana conference in Houston this spring. Perhaps they didn't identify with the militantly feminist thrust of this conference.

Their document contains a whole series of factual errors. They state on page 3: "During the period 1964-1967 the party did not have any position on the Huelga movement. For that matter, the party has not had a position on the Mexican-American question to this date." That is just not true. We have always had a position of support for the farm workers' struggle that goes back before 1964 to the 1930s and 1940s.

On the second point, George Breitman made an important observation in an article in 1969 entitled, "Black Nationalism,

Class Struggle and Party History," that our positions and analysis are developed in our press and literature and not just in formal convention resolutions. Our analysis neither begins nor ends with the adoption of a line resolution. Our participation in the actual struggle over the past several years and our general theoretical understanding of the national question has made the present resolution possible. Further experience will deepen our understanding and further round out our line. That is the only realistic and Marxist approach to the relation between theory and practice.

One of their most barren contributions is the Proletarian Orientation tendency's schematic conception of the universities, the state colleges, the junior colleges, and the high schools. The latter two, they say, have proletarian Chicanos, while the four-year institutions have what they refer to as "the most privileged and most bourgeoisified within the community." "These elements are susceptible to the most blatant petty-bourgeois dilettantism."

They *falsely* claim that we are for orienting only to these four-year institutions, although, according to them, only one-half of one percent of Chicano youth are to be found there. First of all, do they consider the historic San Francisco State strike in 1968 and 1969 at a four-year institution and the Third World Liberation Front strike at U.C. Berkeley, another four-year institution, to be examples of petty-bourgeois dilettantism? This, by the way, was the reason the Black Panthers gave at that time for abstaining from these militant struggles which mobilized significant layers of the Black and Raza communities. These struggles paved the way for Merritt College and without them a Chicano studies department would not have been formed there at that time. Not having fetishes about the size or the supposed class compositions of bourgeois educational institutions, we were able to retain a flexible attitude and use political criteria for intervening first at San Francisco State, then at U.C. Berkeley, then at Merritt, and soon after in the Oakland High School Chicano blowout in the fall of 1969.

This tendency tries to make a case against the four-year institutions in favor of the two-year junior colleges, on the basis of dissimilar Raza enrollment. This is a sterile conception. If that were the case we should have abandoned Merritt College long ago. At the new Hill Campus there are only 50 Chicanos. At the Grove Street site, where a protracted struggle took place this spring for community control, there are only about 150 Chicanos.

Yet at the University of California in Berkeley there are 625 Chicano students. But we didn't abandon Merritt, because it is a *political question* where one intervenes and not just a numbers game.

One of the serious problems at Merritt College, which generally prevails on two-year campuses, is that some 15 to 20 percent drop out during the fall quarter and during the spring quarter some 40 percent drop out. About 30 percent transfer to four-year institutions. This high turnover rate makes continuity in work and activity with Chicano students more difficult.

These are concrete problems which the "Third World Work" counterresolution doesn't mention in relation to important achievements at Merritt College. Among these achievements have been the building of two Northern California Chicano Moratoriums, the Raza contingent to the November 15, 1969, antiwar demonstrations, support to the Oakland High School Chicano blowout, and the building of the community-based Raza Unida Party in the East Oakland barrio—all of which we played an important role in building. Contrary to the statement on page 6 of the counterresolution, the Northern California Raza Unida Party did not just "spring up" but was the result of two years of consistent work and propagandizing at Merritt and in the Chicano struggle as a whole.

One of their most serious errors is the evaluation of the September 16 mass action in East Los Angeles and our role in it. The document contends, "All it showed was the Chicano community trailing behind the gubernatorial candidate of the Democratic Party." Quite to the contrary, it was a militant outpouring of Raza youth, though under a reformist leadership which attempted to blunt the militancy through tight monitoring to prevent people from joining the march, and by inviting the California state Democratic leader Jesse Unruh and the navy to have floats. Without our participation we can confidently say that even *that* action, with all its limitations, would not have taken place.

Another serious factual error is their evaluation of what occurred in Crystal City and how the Raza Unida Party was formed there. In their attempt to make reality fit their schematic view of how they would have liked to have seen it take place, they say the following: "A combination of both high school blow-outs over racist practices and a labor struggle at a nearby Del Monte plant merged not only to politicalize but guide the predominantly

Chicano community in organizing the Raza Unida Party."
Unfortunately for our misnamed Proletarian Orientation tendency, it all began around the demand of Chicanos to elect their own
homecoming queen and elect their cheerleaders. This demand
raised the whole question of who controlled the schools which led
to a confrontation between the entire Chicano community and
the racist Anglo power structure.

It was in the process of this struggle over democratic demands
around community control of the schools that the Chicano
workers became radicalized. The victories of the Raza Unida
Party in April 1970 further inspired them, and *imitating the
student youth* they began "taking care of business" at the
workplace. They didn't look around to see who had been rooted in
the cannery for the last fifteen years to be their leader. Instead
they elected José Angel Gutiérrez, a graduate from a four-year
bourgeois institution with a master's degree and with no other
credentials than having led a student strike to its logical
conclusion and victory!

If these workers had read the "Third World Work" counterresolution they would have known to expect "only the most blatant
petty-bourgeois dilettantism." The developments in Crystal City
confirm our analysis of the present radicalization 100 percent and
prove that the drafters of the counterresolution do not understand
the dynamic of the nationalist struggle. In spite of their protests
the logic of their position leads them away from our analysis of
Chicano nationalism and the combined character of the third
American revolution.

Current Debates in the Movement

Since our convention in 1969, a series of key questions has
emerged or taken on added importance in discussions within the
Chicano movement. One of the most important is the question of
the war in Indochina. The war remains the central political
question to which revolutionaries have to address themselves on
a world scale. The growth of the antiwar movement and the
deepening of antiwar sentiment have helped to create the climate
for the Chicano moratoriums which have taken place over the
past year and a half. After the August 29, 1970, National Chicano
Moratorium, which was the largest mobilization of an oppressed
nationality to date against the war, the moratorium leadership,
under the pressure of the ruling class attack and the influence of
the Communist Party, retreated from united-front mass mobiliza-

tions against the war. However, other sections of the Chicano movement have begun to understand the importance of mass actions against the war, particularly in relation to building the Raza Unida parties. The successful mobilization of 4,000 Chicanos and Latinos in the Raza contingent in the April 24, 1971, antiwar action in San Francisco testifies to the potential for mobilizing the Chicano community in antiwar demonstrations that could surpass the August 29 Chicano Moratorium. In addition Corky Gonzáles recently addressed 700 Black and Chicano GIs at the base named after the notorious Mexican and Indian killer, Fort Kit Carson!

We must consciously understand the significance of these events in order to enlist the support of Chicano activists in building antiwar actions. During the fall of 1968 and the spring of 1969 extremely important struggles took place around the demands for Chicano studies and open enrollment, in which we played an important role. This continues to be an issue that generates controversy and leads to broader struggles over Chicano control of the Chicano community.

The question of Chicanas as women, which was tentatively discussed at the first two Chicano Youth Liberation conferences in Denver, has now emerged as a full-blown issue and is rapidly becoming a major point of discussion and debate within the Chicano movement. The deepening of nationalist consciousness among Chicanos and the development of the women's liberation movement have helped to spark feminist consciousness among Chicanas and Latinas. The appearance of such Chicana newspapers as *El Grito del Norte* and the Conferencia de las Mujeres por La Raza are all indications of a growing feminist consciousness among Chicanas.

Certain leaders within the Chicano movement tend to view the women's liberation movement as a "gringa thing" and are suspicious and hostile toward developing Chicana feminism. But as the resolution "Toward a Mass Feminist Movement" points out, feminism and nationalism are complementary. Feminism leads Chicanas to discover their worth as human beings and therefore strengthens their confidence and desire to struggle against all forms of oppression they face. The national campaign for repeal of all antiabortion laws will play an important role in sharpening the debate which is now being started, and by involving Chicanas in actions against their oppression as women, deepen Chicana feminism.

A National Raza Unida Party

At the recent Chicano Youth Liberation Conference in Denver, the idea of a national Raza Unida Party was raised and a conference was projected for November 1971, to discuss the possibilities of forming one. In viewing this question several things have to be taken into consideration. First is the current strength—and size—of the local and state Raza Unida parties and the existence of a developing leadership and apparatus which can function on a national scale. It is not possible simply to declare a national party into existence. Its growth must flow from the actual strength and consciousness of the parties as they are in real life. The crisis of leadership has not revealed itself as severely within the Chicano movement as in the Black community, but nevertheless, the number of Raza nationalists who understand the need to break with capitalist politics is still limited.

José Angel Gutiérrez expressed the opinion that the task now before the Raza Unida parties is to organize statewide, strengthen their apparatuses, and get on the ballot statewide for 1972. This would be a great step forward for the Raza Unida Party and is the prerequisite for a viable national organization to be launched.

The 1972 presidential elections will put every Raza Unida Party leadership to the test. The maneuvers of McGovern and other slick Kennedy-type liberal Democratic Party politicians will bring tremendous pressure on these new independent formations to come back into the Democratic Party fold, if not on the local level, at least on the state or national level. Support to the Democratic Party in 1972 would be a serious setback to the development of independent Raza Unida parties and greatly miseducate the Chicano people as to who their oppressors and enemies really are.

Tasks of the SWP

The resolution presents a realistic and rounded set of tasks for the party in the coming period. The resolution states: "In aiding the development of an independent mass Chicano movement, the Socialist Workers Party must help popularize the ideas of and help in other ways to build the Chicano parties, the Chicano antiwar movement, the high school and college struggles, and other important actions, including the farm workers' and boycott movements, the struggles of Raza women, the developing movement of Chicano prisoners, and the defense of victims of political frame-ups."

The 1972 SWP election campaign will present a unique opportunity to carry our program to thousands of Chicanos and play an important role in the fight to maintain the independence of the Raza Unida parties in opposition to the Democratic and Republican parties and whatever New Politics formations or tickets the CP and various liberals or muddleheaded radicals may conjure up. Our election campaigns will serve as an excellent model for Raza Unida Party activists of how to utilize the electoral arena to advance the struggle. Carrying out these tasks is the responsibility of the entire party and not solely the job of our Raza comrades. It is important for revolutionary socialists to understand and help provide leadership for the Chicano movement.

Since the 1963 "Freedom Now" resolution we have had a very rich discussion on the national question in relation to the Black population in the United States. This theoretical and practical preparation has been of singular importance in enabling us to understand and participate in the present radicalization. We must now begin a similar process in relation to the history of the Chicano people. This is not only a matter of making contributions to the Chicano struggle, but also involves learning from it. The rich experience of struggle of the Chicano people against their oppression is not only an important, but an essential, chapter in the history of the working class of the United States. This history as well as the fresh lessons which we are gathering will greatly enrich our understanding of, and activity in, all the other mass movements, including, for example, the Puerto Rican movement.

Among our major campaigns this fall will be the antiwar actions November 6. Where possible we should support or help organize the September 16 Chicano Moratoriums against the war which were projected in Denver this past June. The national abortion law repeal campaign will play an important role in mobilizing and linking up with the emerging Chicana feminists who can be expected to have as much impact on the Chicano movement as the women's liberation movement has had on the nation as a whole. We will also be giving support to the developing Raza Unida parties. With the kind of unprecedented election campaign we are projecting, plus the *Militant*'s increased circulation throughout the Southwest, we can confidently predict important gains.

To maximize our ability to take advantage of the opportunities before us, we will be doing a number of things. We have the immediate perspective of strengthening our press coverage and the national coordination and direction of our Chicano work. We want to increase the writing and publication of our general literature on the Chicano struggle, which plays an especially important educational role.

We also hope to be able to increase our collaboration with our Mexican cothinkers, demonstrating the kind of internationalism that is necessary to advance the Chicano struggle. One concrete area of collaboration will be defense of the political prisoners in Mexico and throughout Latin America.

In conclusion, let me quote the final paragraph of the resolution, which summarizes our perspectives on the revolutionary party and the struggle for Chicano liberation: "The mass revolutionary socialist party we seek to build must be multinational as well as proletarian in composition, uniting revolutionary Marxists from the different nationalities in this country into a single, centralized combat party. At the present stage of building such a party, the recruitment and training of cadres is our foremost task. More and more Chicano activists will join the SWP as they come to see the need for a socialist revolution and for a Leninist party to lead that revolution to victory, a party with a correct program on all aspects of the anticapitalist struggle, which unconditionally supports the fight of the Chicano people for self-determination, fights alongside them for their full liberation, and for the full liberation of all humanity."

La migra raid on Mario Cantú's restaurant, July 1976

August 1974 antideportation demonstration in Los Angeles

Mexican Independence Day Parade, Los Angeles, September 1974

August 1976 San Antonio antideportation rally to defend Mario Cantú

The Crisis of American Capitalism and the Struggle for Chicano Liberation

This resolution was adopted at the SWP's Twenty-seventh National Convention in August 1976.

A powerful movement against the superexploitation of Chicanos by American capitalism emerged in the 1960s. The nation's second largest oppressed nationality launched a series of social struggles. These included the fight for bilingual-bicultural education; the drive by Chicano farm workers to organize agribusiness in the Southwest; the movement to regain stolen lands; the fight for more political rights and control over institutions in the Chicano community; the formation of Raza Unida parties. The radicalization of an oppressed people who are overwhelmingly proletarian had begun.

In the decade and a half since that awakening the Chicano movement has gained valuable experience that will help guide future battles. But the movement today faces new challenges stemming from the changed international and national context in which its struggles are unfolding. The upsurge of the Chicano movement began before the 1971 wage freeze, before the meat shortage, the oil crisis, the shock of double-digit inflation, before Watergate, before the 1974-75 depression with double-digit unemployment, and before the new ruling class drive to cut social services to the bone.

The first wave of struggles in the late 1960s and early 1970s won important concessions such as increased educational opportunities, bilingual ballots in some elections, better wages and working conditions for the farm workers organized in the UFW. Today even those gains are under attack. And the chronic problems faced by the Chicano people, far from improving, are growing worse. They, like the other oppressed national minorities, are forced to bear a disproportionate burden of the effects of the economic crisis and the employers' offensive.

Chicanos suffer a dual oppression. They are discriminated against because of race, culture, and language. And as part of the working class they are exploited as wage labor. Chicanos are second class citizens in U.S. society. Higher unemployment levels, lower wages, minimal job security, substandard housing, higher mortality rates, racist education that produces high levels of illiteracy, a virtual absence of Chicano representation at all government levels—such are the facts of Chicano life. These conditions will continue to precipitate struggles and generate demands the U.S. rulers will find increasingly difficult to meet.

This resolution aims to assess the state of the Chicano movement as it faces this new period. It stands on "The Struggle for Chicano Liberation," adopted by the 1971 convention of the Socialist Workers Party, and on "Prospects for Socialism in America," adopted by the 1975 convention. The resolutions affirm the SWP's unconditional support to the struggle for Chicano self-determination, up to and including the right to a separate country if the Chicano people so decide. The 1971 resolution assesses the progressive role of the new rise of Chicano nationalism and draws the balance sheet on the first wave of Chicano struggles. Together with "Prospects for Socialism in America," it discusses the main elements of a program that can orient the Chicano people in a successful fight for political and economic emancipation from U.S. capitalism.

This current resolution concentrates on what has changed since 1971, what is new and what is to be learned from the struggles of the last five years.

The Chicano Movement Today

The militant resurgence of Chicano nationalism is rooted in significant changes that began during World War II and continued throughout the postwar period. The last thirty-five years have witnessed a migration of Chicanos from the rural areas into the urban centers, their incorporation into the industrial working class, and a significant growth of the Chicano population brought about by the immigration of large numbers of Mexican workers.

The Chicano movement emerged under the impact of profound national and international events that shaped the worldwide youth radicalization of the 1960s. Chicanos, like youth and Blacks, were deeply affected and inspired by the advances of the colonial revolutions, particularly the Cuban revolution. At the same time, the success of the civil rights movement and the rise of Black nationalist consciousness had a major impact on Chicanos.

Chicanos benefited directly from the mass struggles of Blacks during this period. The gains won by the civil rights movement and the concessions made by the capitalists in the wake of the 1964-67 Black ghetto uprisings were to one degree or another extended to the Chicano population. This occurred *without* their having to mobilize on the same scale that the Black population did to force these concessions. The gains helped to spur Chicanos into a struggle against their *own* specific oppression and exploitation. While Chicanos learned from the example of the Black struggle, several important differences should be noted.

• Chicanos are bound by a common language that is different from the language of their oppressors. Estimates vary, but probably as much as one-half of the Chicano population view Spanish as their primary language. The stifling of the Spanish language and the related cultural oppression are central to the maintenance of Chicanos as second class citizens. This issue sparked militant struggles in the Chicano community even before the Chicano high school blowouts in several southwestern cities in 1968-69.

• More than 85 percent of the Chicano population live in a well-defined geographical area of the country—the southwestern states of Arizona, New Mexico, Colorado, California, and Texas, sometimes referred to as Aztlán. They are bound by history, culture, and language to both Mexico and the United States.

• Chicanos are the victims of the racist immigration policies of the U.S. ruling class. Harassment and deportation of Mexicanos working in the U.S. without immigration visas is standard government policy, aimed at discouraging Mexicano and Chicano workers from organizing or fighting to improve their lot. Such racist policies are designed to intimidate the entire Chicano population.

These and other aspects of their oppression help determine the character of the Chicanos as a unique people distinct from any other oppressed national grouping in the United States. They also determine the axes of the struggles that have given rise to a new generation of militant Chicano fighters.

A focal point of the Chicano movement from the mid-1960s to the present has been the organizing by the farm workers, led by César Chávez. From its inception, the farm workers saw their movement as a social movement combining the fight for social justice for the superexploited *campesinos* with the drive to win collective bargaining rights and union benefits.

Together with the New Mexico land-grant movement, *la causa*—the cause, as the farm workers call their movement— forced the plight of Chicanos into the public eye and marked their social and political awakening as a people. This effort provided the initial impulses for the Chicano radicalization. The farm workers have won broad support for their fight among students, Blacks, Puerto Ricans, women, unionists, and other working people. Such solidarity has helped to demonstrate that the enemy is the same and points toward the need to organize and mobilize all working people to replace capitalism with socialism.

Opposition to the imperialist war in Vietnam, spurred by the high casualty rates for Chicano GIs, fueled the militancy and combativity of the Chicano people. Chicanos mobilized by the tens of thousands in several important actions against the war. The most significant was the National Chicano Moratorium in August 1970, when 30,000 Chicanos demonstrated in East Los Angeles. These demonstrations had a profound impact on the Chicano people, the rulers' attitude toward them, and the course of the opposition to the war.

By linking the imperialist war in Vietnam to the oppression Chicanos suffer in the United States, these antiwar actions countered the lies peddled by the capitalist media that Chicanos, Blacks, other oppressed groups, and working people in general had nothing to gain from joining the antiwar movement, which they tried to portray as a white, middle class student movement. The Chicano mobilizations helped to inspire the development of similar actions in the Black community, although not of the same massive size. They also helped deepen consciousness among Chicanos of the need to oppose U.S. imperialism in the colonial and semicolonial world.

Chicano activists became more interested in political developments in these countries, particularly Latin America. This interest has deepened over the last five years. Many have rallied to the defense of Latin American political prisoners, demonstrated against U.S. support to the bloody Chilean junta, joined actions demanding "U.S. Hands Off Angola," and other similar protests against U.S. imperialist ventures. Awakening internationalism among Chicanos has been reflected in growing interest and collaboration between Chicanos and the Mexican student and workers' movements, and stronger ties to the struggles of Puerto Ricans both in the United States and in Puerto Rico.

Chicana Feminism

The emergence of the women's movement at the crest of the radicalization of the 1960s and the continuing spread of feminist ideas has also had a deep impact on the Chicano struggle, especially on Chicanas. The triple oppression Chicanas face because of sex, nationality, and class places them among the most impoverished and least educated sections of the American population.

Chicanas receive miserably low wages. A study of government income figures in 1973, before the worst of the economic crisis, showed that nearly 50 percent of all Chicanas employed that year earned *less than $2,000.* Nearly 75 percent of Chicana workers in 1973 had incomes under $4,000.

The feminist and nationalist struggles of the last decade have spurred the development of Chicana feminist organizations in opposition to the racist practice of forced sterilization and in support of the right to safe and legal abortions. Chicanas are beginning to participate in united-front activities with other women for the ratification of the Equal Rights Amendment, against cutbacks in child care and other social services, and against attacks on affirmative action programs.

At the same time, heightened feminist consciousness among Chicanas has had a major effect on the Chicano movement as a whole. Four or five years ago Chicanas had to fight against exclusion from the leadership bodies of Chicano movement organizations. While they still have to argue with Chicano male leaders who oppose feminism as a "white women's thing" that is supposedly divisive and irrelevant to the Chicano struggle, in the last several years a striking change has taken place. Many of the Raza Unida parties and Chicano student organizations have included demands for women's rights in their platforms and have Chicana commissions or caucuses. The United Farm Workers have a growing number of Chicanas as prominent spokespeople as well as organizers of the boycott movement. Several important Chicana conferences have been held in recent years to discuss the issues facing Chicanas, and this spread of feminist ideas can be expected to continue to influence the Chicano movement.

Their third class economic and social status in American society gives the struggles of Chicanas against their oppression as women an explosive character.

Chicano Students

Another important component in the struggles of Chicanos in the last fifteen years has been the Chicano student movement. Chicano college and high school students registered important gains through their struggles for bilingual-bicultural education and more high school rights, and through fights for open admissions, Chicano studies, and hiring of more Chicano faculty and staff.

Chicano students remain the most radicalized layer of the Chicano population, although today they are less organized than five years ago. The MEChAs (Movimiento Estudiantil Chicano de Aztlán—Chicano Student Movement of Aztlán), MAYOs (Mexican-American Youth Organization), and UMASes (United Mexican-American Students) helped to organize and mobilize support for the farm workers, undocumented Mexicano workers and other Chicano community struggles. They played a role in popularizing the concept of independent Chicano political action and helped launch the Raza Unida parties, the most advanced political organizations yet to emerge out of the Chicano struggles.

Over the last five years the Chicano student movement has been weakened by a crisis of perspectives and leadership, and many of the Chicano student groups have retreated into becoming social clubs. The statewide MAYO in Texas, for example, no longer exists. Others have been drawn into community "poverty" programs sponsored and funded by government agencies. Still others were drawn into sectarian political schemes. No student organization has yet emerged from these recent experiences with a perspective of organizing and mobilizing the masses of Chicano students around clear and concrete demands that are fought for on every level, from actions in the streets to the building of the Raza Unida parties as mass Chicano political parties independent of and opposed to the two parties of capitalist rule in this country.

But the government's growing offensive against the rights and gains of Chicano students has begun to encounter resistance and to revitalize the Chicano student movement. A number of conferences held over the last year have drawn Chicano students into discussions and debates on how to move the Chicano struggle forward in the face of this racist offensive, despite differences on other questions. Chicano students are once again beginning to play a bigger role in campus struggles against budget cuts, and in organizing student support for the Coors beer boycott and the UFW-called boycotts of lettuce, grapes, and Gallo wines. Another indication of this increased activity among Chicano students is their role in building a response to cop killings of Chicano youth in National City and San José, California, in the spring of 1976.

The Economic Crisis

The 1960s were a decade of unprecedented capitalist prosperity and expansion, which incorporated growing numbers of Chicanos into the work force. It brought a rising standard of living for many of the most oppressed. Yet even under these conditions, Chicano unemployment in 1969 officially stood at 6 percent (nearly double the national average for whites). Median Chicano family income was less than 70 percent of that for Anglos.

Despite any temporary upturns, American capitalism has entered a long-term period of economic crisis and stagnation. The future will generally see higher, not lower, unemployment levels; high inflation rates; fewer, not more, social services; falling, not rising, standards of living for working people.

In keeping with a centuries-old policy of divide and rule, the American ruling class will make every effort to shift a disproportionate burden of this economic crisis onto the Chicano population.

They will attempt to derail struggles against the deteriorating living standards of all American workers, Anglo and Chicano alike, by fostering racist and xenophobic attitudes that deepen the divisions they have created in the working class. These will be used to bolster the reactionary idea that a lion's share of the crisis *should* be borne by Chicanos and other oppressed nationalities, and that social, economic, and political advances they have made through struggle in recent years *should* be rolled back.

The ruling class will make sure that the cutbacks in social services hurt Chicanos more than Anglos: more hospitals will be closed in Chicano areas than Anglo; more schools will cut out bilingual programs than programs vital to Anglos; rising costs for basic necessities like food, housing, water, heat, light, transportation, health care, will take a bigger bite out of Chicano incomes than Anglo; public transportation systems will be reduced more in Chicano areas than Anglo, welfare cutbacks will affect a larger portion of the Chicano population than of the Anglo; regressive taxes will take a larger chunk of Chicano budgets than of Anglo, etc., etc.

A 1974 government report on low-income Americans and poverty in the United States showed that 12 percent of the total population had incomes below the official poverty level. At the same time, approximately 23 percent of what the government statisticians call "people of Spanish origin" fell below the poverty line. The real situation is even worse than those figures indicate since the government camouflages the full picture by lumping Chicanos into a catchall category of "Hispanic-Americans" that covers all Latinos, including those who have a relatively higher standard of living than Chicanos or Puerto Ricans.

The impact of the economic crisis will make itself felt with particular acuteness in three areas, each of which has already generated important struggles: the fight for jobs and against discriminatory hiring and layoff practices; the fight against deportations and racist immigration policies; and the fight for an equal education, a bilingual-bicultural education.

1. Jobs

Chronically high Chicano unemployment rates have risen dramatically under the impact of the 1974-75 depression. Joblessness among the Latino work force officially rose from 8.2 percent in the fourth quarter of 1974 to 11.8 percent in the same quarter of 1975. But these statistics do not include the tens of thousands of Chicanos who are simply not counted because they have never before been in the work force and don't qualify for unemployment benefits. Nor do they count the large number of Chicanos who are underemployed in part-time or seasonal jobs, or those who have given up looking for work. The real picture can be seen in the fact that overall unemployment in the Chicano barrio of East Los Angeles is estimated to be closer to 45 percent, and as high as 60 percent among Chicano youth.

The disproportionately high unemployment rates in the Chicano barrios pose two interrelated issues: the right to a job, and the struggle against discriminatory hiring and layoff practices which double the burden of unemployment borne by Chicano workers.

The fight for jobs—a struggle that has not yet been taken up in any serious way by the leadership of the U.S. labor movement despite the high unemployment rates of recent years—revolves around two basic demands. One is the need for an emergency government-financed public works program to create millions of socially useful jobs. Among the projects involved could be the construction in the Chicano community of decent, low-cost housing; hospitals, health care and child care centers, schools, mass transit systems, parks, recreation centers, and other needed social services.

The second demand is for a shortening of the workweek with no cut in pay. This would spread the available work and help guarantee everyone a job. These are the measures behind which the labor movement as a whole, including Chicanos, must mobilize if the rulers are to be prevented from pushing through massive cutbacks in social services and shifting the burden of the economic crisis onto the backs of the working class. Especially in industries and areas where Chicanos are numerically strong, the Chicano movement must raise such issues, explain them, and demand that the entire labor movement fight for them.

Chicano workers face an additional problem. Discriminatory employment practices are consciously and systematically used by the capitalists to divide and weaken the working class as a whole, and to maintain a low-cost labor pool that can be utilized to drive down the wages of all workers.

In recent years significant gains have been won by Chicano and other minority workers through struggles that established preferential hiring, promotion, and training programs that opened previously closed job opportunities to Chicano workers. The massive layoffs in the 1974-75 depression were often used to wipe out affirmative action gains. Chicano, Black, Puerto Rican, and women workers became the first victims of the bosses' racist and sexist employment practices.

Special measures are required to fight the job discrimination imposed by generations of racist discrimination. This is doubly true in periods of economic crisis when the employers try to take advantage of the high unemployment to drive back any gains made by the most oppressed sections of the working class. Chicanos should join with Black and Puerto Rican workers, women workers, and others who see the need for class solidarity against the employers' attempts to divide the workers along race and sex lines. They should demand that, when layoffs do occur, the bosses should not be permitted to utilize the layoffs to reduce the percentage of Chicano, Black, and women workers, the most vulnerable victims of discriminatory employment practices.

The struggle against discriminatory layoffs has already generated a number of important battles, including one currently under way at Kelly Air Force Base in San Antonio, Texas. An estimated 70 percent of the Chicanos employed there are threatened with layoffs. Court action is being taken against the U.S. Air Force, the Department of Defense, and the Air Force Logistics Command to halt the racist moves.

The fight against discriminatory layoffs is a precondition to establishing the elementary ties of class solidarity within the labor movement, based on support for the needs of the most oppressed and exploited layers of the working class. It is the only way to combat the racist divisions within the working class that are fostered by the employers, who try to convince the relatively privileged worker that his individual need of a job can be solved only if someone else—one of "them"—gets laid off instead of him.

The fight against discriminatory layoffs also poses the need to transform the unions into organizations of class struggle that fight for their members' needs and champion the demands of all the oppressed, both on and off the job. The bureaucratic misleaders of the trade unions today base themselves on the most privileged white workers. Far from defending the oppressed sectors of the working class, far from fighting the discriminatory layoffs, they have by and large taken a stand of defending the seniority system to justify the firing of disproportionately large numbers of Chicano workers. It should be remembered that the seniority system itself was an earlier victory won through struggles by working people to prevent the bosses from arbitrarily firing whomever they please. Today the labor movement has to prevent the capitalists from perverting the principle of seniority to strengthen the rulers' racist hiring practices.

2. Immigration and Deportation

Closely linked to the struggle against job discrimination is the fight against racist immigration policies that have resulted in the deportation of hundreds of thousands of Mexicano, Central American, and Caribbean workers without immigration visas.

The Immigration and Naturalization Service (INS) of the Justice Department, which has an interest in hiding the real facts in order to bolster its racist drive, estimates that there are between 6 and 8 million workers in the United States without papers. One to 4 million of these "illegal aliens," the INS claims, cross or are brought across the U.S. borders yearly in search of better jobs. Of these, 85 to 90 percent come from Mexico.

While accurate data is not available, some government statisticians estimate that undocumented workers today comprise close to 8 percent of the total U.S. work force. The majority of these workers are concentrated in the garment and textile industries, rubber and plastics, stone and clay, cosmetics, furniture, food processing, and footwear. Others are involved in the manufacture of some metals, laundry services, railroad transportation, and construction. Virtually all are in the lowest-paying, unskilled categories of these industries. American agribusiness remains one of the major employers of Mexicano workers, both with and without papers.

Mexican immigration has always been an important factor in the Chicano work force, and in the Chicano population as a whole. It has helped to swell the ranks of the Chicano nationality and constantly reinforces the cultural and historical ties between Chicanos and their Mexican brothers and sisters.

In the early part of this century, Mexican immigration was encouraged by the U.S. capitalists in order to provide a cheap source of labor in their fields and textile mills. Semicolonial conditions in Mexico facilitated this emigration.

During the Second World War, expanded war production drew many of the nation's farmers and farm workers into cities and into basic industry. At the same time, agricultural production was undergoing a rapid growth, and growers feared that the elimination of the large surplus labor pool in the countryside would drive up wages and create conditions more favorable to unionization of agricultural labor. This led to a negotiated contract between the Mexican government and the United States under which the Roosevelt administration contracted for the importation of Mexicano workers to fill the needs of American agribusiness. The Bracero Program, as the contract was named, legally brought nearly half a million Mexicans into the U.S. to work on the farms at slave wages, plus a special consignment of

80,000 to work on the section gangs and maintenance crews of the railroads. Between 1943 and 1947, the U.S. government shelled out a total of $120 million to the Mexican government in payment for the Mexicano labor. This program was not officially ended until 1964.

Racist immigration practices are not new; they have been a constant element in American history since the first shipload of Black slaves arrived. They have intensified during every period of social and economic crisis in the United States. Historically, Mexican immigration, unlike European immigration, has been used by the U.S. rulers as a source of *temporary* cheap labor—to be encouraged when the labor market is tight and more hands are needed in order to keep the wage levels down; to be deported to the Mexican side of the border when jobs are scarce. The capitalists also use spectacular massive deportations of workers who are no longer needed as a way of fostering racist and xenophobic attitudes. They try to make it look as if the Mexicanos without papers are the cause of unemployment, and the government is helping to alleviate the economic difficulties of American workers. Chicanos and other Latinos are harassed in these racist dragnet raids, whether or not they are citizens.

Today, the capitalists attempt to paint a picture of hordes of Mexicans swooping across the border to steal American jobs. The bourgeois media publish article after article claiming these undocumented workers end up on welfare, receive unemployment benefits, use public hospitals, put their children in local schools, and take advantage of other social services, thus burdening "citizen" workers with heavier taxes. The lies of this racist campaign are exposed by the facts. For example, a study by the INS reveals that of nearly 200,000 Mexicanos working without visas, who were apprehended in 1975, 132,000 made less than $2.50 an hour, and most were working in the fields. When the bosses were offered unemployed U.S. workers at the guaranteed minimum wage to replace the deported "illegals," the most common response was hearty laughter. While the "illegal" workers are forced to pay taxes, they receive virtually none of the benefits, such as social security, unemployment compensation, and social services. The "illegal" is clearly the victim of economic injustice, not the cause.

Deportations have escalated to monstrous proportions over the last five years, with almost daily raids by *la migra* into the Chicano barrios. In addition to the deportations, the U.S.

Congress is considering a variety of bills designed to infringe further on the rights of these workers as well as those of Chicanos. The Rodino bill would fine employers who "knowingly hire" workers without papers and empower the U.S. attorney general to issue citizenship identification papers for employers' use. This would be a step toward the introduction of internal passports which Chicanos and others of Latin American descent would have to produce in order to get a job. These legislative proposals simply provide one more excuse for racists to deny employment to Chicanos. They are a major threat to the civil liberties of all American citizens.

Along with racist hiring and layoff practices, the bosses' policies on "illegals" are supported by much of the trade union bureaucracy. The AFL-CIO is officially on record in favor of the deportation of undocumented workers, who are supposedly taking jobs away from Americans. The demands by labor officials to deport workers without papers are a coverup for their refusal to organize and lead a fight in defense of the living standards of all workers. As it becomes clearer to the ranks of the trade unions that such policies do not protect even existing jobs and living standards, increasing numbers of workers will begin to see a need to fight to change the reactionary anti–working-class policies of the labor bureaucracy and install a class-struggle perspective and leadership in its stead.

International labor solidarity is fundamental to unifying and defending the entire working class, its gains, and its organizations. The right to move freely back and forth across the border, the right to work in the United States when and where one chooses, without fear of harassment because of lack of work papers or immigration documents, is one of the demands at the very heart of the Chicano movement.

Struggles by Chicano workers both on the job and as part of the broad Chicano movement will play a key role in helping to reverse the class-collaborationist and racist positions of the current misleaders of the American labor movement and mobilize a mass movement of the Chicano people and their allies to halt the deportations. A mass antideportation movement that could organize actions in defense of Mexicanos and other immigrants without visas has the potential of drawing in not only Chicanos, other workers, civil libertarians, and students, but of mobilizing workers without papers in defense of their rights.

3. Education

The racist and inferior education Chicanos receive in U.S. schools aids the bosses in maintaining a large section of Chicano workers as part of the reserve pool of low-cost labor. Above all, suppression of the Spanish language is used to reinforce general racist policies and to perpetuate the unequal status of Chicanos in American society.

The education meted out to Chicanos guarantees that a large proportion of the Chicano population cannot speak, write, or read well in either English or Spanish. Lack of proficiency in the English language is then used to deny Chicanos better-paying jobs, and to justify the disproportionate joblessness among Chicanos, the miserable housing and wretched living conditions they are forced to suffer. Moreover, by promoting the English language and Euro-American culture as superior to the language and culture of Chicanos, the rulers foster chauvinist sentiments among Anglo workers. Chicanos are portrayed as un-American, deserving what they get because they are unwilling to learn English.

Even the federal government's civil rights commission estimates that more than five million American students are in need of special language programs. The majority of these are Chicano and Puerto Rican youth. This lack of adequate bilingual-bicultural education results in a high push out rate for Chicano students. More than 40 percent of those who enter the first grade never graduate from high school. Compared with 12.0 school years completed by whites, the median is 8.1 for Chicanos.

This situation has given rise to massive struggles by Chicanos for equal education. When thousands of Chicano high school students in East Los Angeles launched strikes in their schools in the blowouts of 1968, they demanded "Education, Not Eradication!" This demand captured the deep desire of Chicano students for an education that touches the history of Chicanos, that respects their culture, language, and heritage, and that isn't designed to force Chicanos to assimilate into Anglo society and culture.

In the last decade, legal challenges, combined with militant action by Chicano, Puerto Rican, and Chinese parents and students, have scored important victories in the fight for bilingual-bicultural education. The most significant was the January 1974 Supreme Court ruling, *Lau* v. *Nichols*, declaring that failure to provide bilingual programs to students with little or no proficiency in English is a denial of equal educational opportunity under Title VI of the 1964 Civil Rights Act. The decision was based on a suit filed by Chinese parents in San Francisco. It came nearly three decades after the First Regional Conference on Education of Spanish-speaking People in the Southwest, which recommended an end to segregated schools for Chicano children, improved teacher training, and better methods in teaching English.

The legal *right* to bilingual education established by the *Lau* decision can have the same significance for Chicanos in their fight for equal education as the 1954 Supreme Court decision on school desegregation has for the Black community.

The fight to fully *implement* bilingual-bicultural education, like the struggle to *enforce* desegregation of the schools, is unfolding in the face of racist attacks and budget cuts, which are axing existing programs. The meaning of the *Lau* decision has recently been challenged by the Department of Health, Education and Welfare in an attempt to retreat from the establishment of bilingual education as a *right* that the government must provide. But the racist offensive against Chicano rights to equal education has begun to generate a response by Chicanos in Denver, Tucson, Dallas, and elsewhere.

Chicanos, like Blacks and other oppressed national minorities, are front-line victims of de facto segregation in American society. There is a long history of Chicano struggles against segregation, not only in education, but in housing and public facilities. Throughout the 1940s and 1950s, Chicano organizations such as the League of United Latin-American Citizens (LULAC), the Alianza Hispano-Americano, and the American Council of Spanish-speaking People engaged in numerous court battles to secure legal equality.

On February 5, 1944, following a local struggle, a federal court in California ruled that Mexican-Americans' rights to equal protection under the law guaranteed by the Fourteenth Amendment were being abridged because they were denied access to the only public swimming pool in San Bernardino, California. The court action waged by Chicano leaders set an important precedent that led to major challenges against segregated public facilities, especially the schools.

These and other court actions by Chicanos were successful in striking down local laws segregating Chicanos, and helped set the stage for the Supreme Court decision in 1954 that declared "separate but equal" to be unconstitutional. They also led to another important high court decision the same year. The American Council of Spanish-speaking People had brought suit to reverse the conviction of a Texas Chicano, Pete Hernández, for murder, by an all-white jury. The Supreme Court ruled that Hernández had been denied a fair trial, and recognized Mexican-Americans as an identifiable ethnic group that suffered systematic discrimination in Texas. These victories, together with the *Lau* decision in 1974, provide the constitutional framework of the struggle against de facto segregation and for equal education, including struggles for bilingual-bicultural education.

Chicanos, Puerto Ricans, Chinese, and others who have the right to bilingual programs are fighting to implement the law by establishing bilingual-bicultural education programs that teach all basic subjects in Spanish or their primary language with teachers who are bilingual and respect the culture and heritage of the students, and administrative staffs that are sensitive to the needs of Chicanos and other oppressed minorities. In order to win these programs, Chicanos often have to mobilize even to maintain existing bilingual programs, and the right to attend any school of their choice—including the better-equipped and better-staffed schools in the Anglo communities.

In a cynical attempt to pit Blacks and Chicanos against each other in their fight for equal education, and thus cut across effective collaboration in the struggle for their rights, the capitalist-dominated courts and school boards in a number of cities have consciously devised desegregation busing plans that would destroy existing bilingual-bicultural programs. This has helped to reinforce fears among some Chicanos that busing means an end to whatever gains they have registered in their fight for equal education. Many activists correctly understand that education in the United States is racist to the core, but view busing as the rulers' way of trying to "integrate" Chicanos into schools and a society that will destroy their culture, heritage, and language.

The fight for bilingual-bicultural education and Chicano control over the schools in the Chicano community need not be counterposed to school desegregation through busing. Unfortunately, some Chicano activists have fallen into the trap set by the ruling class to prevent an effective united struggle by *all* victims of racist education on all fronts.

What is involved, both in struggles for Black and Chicano community control and the fight to keep the buses rolling, is the right of the communities of the oppressed nationalities to decide for *themselves* how and by what means they will achieve equality in education. The struggle to desegregate the schools through busing and the fight to maintain and extend bilingual-bicultural education are parts of the same battle and against the same enemy. This is the racist capitalist system, which systematically denies equal education to Chicanos, Blacks, Puerto Ricans, and other oppressed national minorities in order to keep them superexploited.

Where the Chicano community decides that in order to secure equal education they want their children bused to the better schools in all-Anglo communities, demands must be raised to assure that the bilingual-bicultural programs not be eliminated, but expanded, and continue to be available to Chicano students in their new schools, *regardless* of the numbers of Chicanos being bused.

In other cases, the Chicano community may decide to fight for massive funding of schools in their community in order to bring those schools up to the standards of the best schools and to assure adequate bilingual-bicultural, and other special programs, as well as the hiring of sufficient trained personnel to administer such programs.

In Denver, for example, racist forces lined up against court-ordered busing and the court's instructions to immediately implement bilingual-bicultural education in the schools. Antiracist forces in the Chicano and Black communities joined forces in an effort to beat back racist attacks on both of these provisions of the court's order. They fought the racists' attempts to divide the movement when the racists were successful in getting the court to remove the bilingual-bicultural provision from the court order. The united antiracist forces continued to demand implementation of bilingual-bicultural programs, as well as an end to segregated education in Denver.

Chicanos are also faced with dwindling opportunities for a college education. Budget cutbacks and tuition hikes affect Chicano and other minority students most because, in order to attend college, they are forced to rely more on financial aid and scholarship programs. They also need special education programs to help make up for the inferior education Chicanos get in the public schools. Gains that were won in the early 1970s, such as increased admissions to colleges and universities, the establishment of Chicano studies departments, and the hiring of more Chicano professors and administrators, are in danger of being wiped out.

The Chicano movement and other antiracist forces have begun to respond to attacks on bilingual-bicultural education, desegregation, and education budgets. Actions like those in Boston on December 14, 1974, and May 17, 1975, organized to defend the desegregation forces in that embattled city provide important examples of the kind of response Chicanos can organize with others. The National Student Coalition Against Racism, which played a central role in building the May 17 Boston action, has also been instrumental in drawing together, in cities like San Diego, San José, and Denver, those forces willing to fight against police terror in the Chicano community as well as for bilingual-bicultural education and other rights.

As the crisis of capitalism deepens and the racist assault on Chicano rights escalates, it is increasingly clear that concessions won in the past are not permanent. They were wrung out of the capitalists largely as a result of powerful mass actions by Chicanos, Blacks, and Puerto Ricans demanding their rights. Similar actions are necessary in order to defend these gains if Chicanos are to win further advances.

Chicanos and the Labor Movement

Chicano workers have a proud history in trade union battles and in struggles against discrimination on the job. They played a leading role in the battles that unionized the powerful western mining industry. They participated in strikes and demonstrations to organize the rail industry, and were a powerful component of other union struggles in the Southwest. They often paid with their blood for their efforts as the employers, aided by the capitalist government, deported and repatriated thousands of Mexicano and Chicano workers, including those whose families had lived in the Southwest for generations. Nine of the eighteen victims of Rockefeller's 1914 Ludlow massacre were Chicanos.

This militant heritage has not been lost, as Chicano workers today continue to fight for a better standard of living and their full rights on the job and in the unions.

The great bulk of the Chicano work force is employed in such basic industries as steel, auto, mining, railroads, meat packing, electrical, transportation, garment, construction, and agriculture. Chicanos are disproportionately confined to the least skilled, poorest-paying job categories in all of these industries.

The weakness of the organized labor movement throughout the entire Southwest holds down the living standards of all workers. A key challenge that confronts the labor movement today is the need to organize the large numbers of unorganized workers. A significant portion of these nonunionized workers in the Southwest are Chicano.

The garment industry provides an instructive example. Chicanas and Mexicanas are the basic work force in the thousands of sweatshops that dot major southwestern cities. Their working conditions are scandalous, and they often receive wages below the federal minimum standard. These workers naturally turn to the unions as the only organizations that can help them fight for better hours and working conditions, and higher living standards. The two-year strike against the sweatshops of Willie Farah and the boycott of his products offer testimony to this.

The majority-Chicano work force in the Farah pants factories in Texas went out on strike in 1972 to win the basic right to union recognition. Intimidation and harassment did not stop the organizing effort. Taking their cue from the *campesinos,* the garment workers launched a national boycott of Farah pants, appealed to the Chicano community for support and solidarity in the strike and boycott, as well as to students and other potential allies. In 1974, largely as a result of the publicity generated by the boycott, the broad support the workers won for their struggle, and the economic damage the boycott did to Farah, the strike ended in victory. The Farah strike and boycott reflect the deep impact Chicano nationalism has had on Chicano workers.

One indication of the effects of racism inside the labor movement is the fact that while Chicanos comprise more than 30 percent of the steelworkers' union membership in eleven western states, and a large percentage of the steelworkers in the Midwest, there are virtually no high Chicano elected officials in the United Steelworkers. The same discrimination prevails in the United Auto Workers, where Chicanos comprise as much as one-third of the membership in the UAW district encompassing California, Utah, and Arizona.

The Mexican-American Union Council (MAUC) and the Labor Council for Latin American Advancement (LCLAA) are examples of emerging organizations led by Chicano unionists. MAUC is comprised primarily of Chicano steelworkers in Los Angeles, and the LCLAA is made up of lower-level Chicano union functiona- ries from various AFL-CIO unions, the United Auto Workers, and Teamsters. The LCLAA, set up by the AFL-CIO officialdom, is mainly working to organize Chicano unionists to vote for the Democratic Party. However, it has also been forced to pressure the AFL-CIO bureaucracy for more jobs and union positions for Chicanos. The LCLAA has also put some distance between itself and the Meany bureaucracy's reactionary position demanding deportation of undocumented workers. LCLAA supports legisla- tion that calls for a moratorium on deportations.

Chicano unionists more and more often find themselves obliged to take up the social and political issues most affecting the oppressed. The Chicano caucus of the National Education Association, for example, joined with antiracist forces in Denver in 1975 to fight attacks on bilingual-bicultural education, desegregation, and affirmative action in hiring of Chicano and Black education personnel.

These same social and political issues are posed for the entire labor movement, and the struggles of Chicano unionists will be an important factor in educating the union ranks on the interrelationship between the labor movement and these social struggles. They will help to teach other unionists why labor must take up the social, political, and economic demands that Chicanos and other doubly oppressed sectors of the working class are pressing today, if the labor movement as a whole is to effectively counter the divisive tactics of the bosses and organize itself against the capitalist offensive.

The present leadership of the trade unions is the major obstacle to this process. It is a narrow-minded, conservative, racist, and procapitalist bureaucracy that subordinates the needs of the working class to the rulers' attempts to maintain class peace. In fighting to turn their unions into instruments of struggle that defend the interests of all workers, instead of a dwindling number of jobs for a few temporarily more fortunate individuals, the union ranks will discover that the class-collaborationist policies of the current union bureaucracy must be replaced with a policy of militant struggle by the working class on all social, political, and economic fronts. A new union leadership, committed to such a class-struggle course, will emerge in the battles to come.

Struggles by Chicano workers, along with those of other superexploited layers of the working class, will play a vanguard role in this process of developing class and political consciousness in the labor movement, and educating broad layers of workers to think about and act on broader social issues, placing them in a new political context. The disproportionately high layoffs of Chicanos, their continued concentration in the lowest-paying jobs, their lack of representation in decision-making bodies of the unions, and the impact of Chicano nationalism on Chicano workers serve to deepen their class and political consciousness. The struggles by farm workers, the fight for equal education, actions against deportations, and fights for Chicano community control have brought increasing numbers of Chicano workers into motion against their national oppression and class exploitation. Socialist ideas, mass action in the streets, and the need for *political* answers to the problems confronting the working class seem reasonable to many Chicano workers today.

Initiatives in the direction of independent Chicano political action by the Raza Unida parties have helped to break some Chicano workers away from the Democratic Party and educate a layer of Chicano workers on the need for political independence of the entire working class from the political representatives of its capitalist exploiters. The fact that predominantly Chicano union locals of the Amalgamated Clothing Workers, Amalgamated Meat Cutters, International Union of Electrical, Radio and Machine Workers, Retail Clerks, and Service Employees International Union in San Antonio endorsed a Raza Unida Party candidate for state legislature in 1974 is an indication of developments that will take place if a mass independent Chicano political party begins to emerge. The accomplishments of the Crystal City Raza Unida Party have inspired Chicano workers throughout Texas and provide a concrete example on a local scale of what can be achieved through independent Chicano political action.

Such developments are also an indication of the kind of response an independent party of labor would evoke. Such a party, basing itself on the organized union movement and putting forward a program of struggle in the interests of the entire class and its allies, would find an immediate base of support among the most militant and conscious Chicano unionists, who would play a key role in its construction and in charting its direction.

The Farm Workers' Struggle

The fifteen-year long organizing drive by the United Farm Workers union has inspired the entire Chicano movement to fight for justice, and has provided an example to the entire labor movement. Despite its limitations, it has indicated the direction in which the trade unions must move if they are to become transformed into popular organizations of class struggle.

Though a minority of the Chicano work force are employed as agricultural workers, the struggles of farm workers have been and will continue to occupy an important place in the fight for Chicano liberation. The farm workers' movement arose in the midst of a deepgoing radical ferment in the United States and emerged in response to the wretched lot of the majority-Chicano and -Mexicano farm labor force in the Southwest.

Cries of *Justicia!* and *Huelga!* have echoed in California and Texas fields for decades. The chant of the *campesinos, ¡Sí, se puede!*—yes, we can!—expresses the burning commitment of the farm workers to their struggle for justice and their understanding of the challenge before them.

To appreciate the significance of this movement it must be examined in the context of the difficulties in organizing this superexploited sector of the work force. There are three million agricultural workers in the United States. All past attempts to organize farm workers have been brutally crushed. The mechanization and industrialization of agricultural production over the last thirty-five years have transformed the American farm into the most advanced monopoly agribusiness in the world. Organizing these new factories in the fields poses a different and more difficult challenge than organizing a factory within four walls. These problems are aggravated by the increasingly migratory and seasonal character of the agricultural work force.

The drive by the United Farm Workers of America, AFL-CIO, beginning in the mid-1960s, is the most successful organizing effort to date. What differentiates the UFW's efforts from those in the past is its appeal to the nationalist consciousness of the Chicano and Mexicano farm workers, and the character of its drive as a social movement, taking up the many different aspects of oppression affecting the farm workers. *La causa* became the watchword for Chicanos fighting for their rights both in the fields and in the urban barrios. In turn, the resurgence of Chicano nationalism reinforces the fight of the farm workers.

When the California grape growers were forced to sign contracts with the UFW in 1970, it was not only a landmark victory for the thousands of *campesinos* who finally won benefits most industrial workers already enjoyed, but a signal gain for the Chicano people as a whole. This victory was the result of the massive support organized by the UFW through its international grape boycott, which mobilized tens of thousands of Chicanos, unionists, students, and others to force the growers to come to terms with the UFW. In its battle against the wealthy growers, the UFW had to take up the social and political oppression of the farm workers, in addition to their economic exploitation in the fields. It had to look beyond the fields and mobilize its allies among Chicanos and other oppressed and exploited sectors of the population. In doing so, even in a limited way, the UFW leadership transcended the narrow vision of the AFL-CIO officialdom.

If the organizing effort is to be ultimately victorious, the UFW needs to deepen these activities. The farm workers are faced with major obstacles, including many of the same ones that spelled defeat for past organizing efforts. They are up against some of the most powerful monopolies in the world, actively supported by the capitalist government.

At the same time, the UFW is confronted with the shameless strikebreaking activity of the corrupt Teamster bureaucracy, and the unwillingness of the AFL-CIO leadership to back their verbal support for the UFW with the necessary aid to insure a durable victory for the *campesinos*.

The UFW has suffered severe blows since 1970. Along with the struggle in the grape fields, the UFW was on a drive to organize California lettuce workers. With the aid and collaboration of the top leadership of the International Brotherhood of Teamsters, who signed sweetheart contracts behind the backs of striking lettuce workers, the growers began a campaign against the lettuce workers, forcing the UFW to launch a national boycott of head lettuce in 1971.

This was but a preview of a concerted campaign to destroy the UFW. In 1973, the Teamster bureaucracy's alliance with the growers was cemented when they signed sweetheart contracts with grape growers who had refused to renew contracts with the UFW. In response to this outrageous union-busting drive, the UFW called a strike in the grape fields and launched a new nationwide grape boycott in an effort to bring massive public pressure to bear on the growers. The striking farm workers were met with brutal violence by sheriffs' deputies, right-wing vigilantes, and thugs hired by the Teamster leadership. In the summer of 1973, thousands of UFW strikers were arrested and jailed, and pickets were harassed and beaten by goons and cops. The violence culminated in the murder of two striking farm workers in mid-August.

Hit by this murderous repression in the fields and a rapidly dwindling strike fund, the UFW leadership retreated, calling off the picketing in the fields in the fall of 1973. The AFL-CIO Executive Council, which had donated $1.6 million to the union to carry out its strike in the spring of that year, failed to come through with further financial support. The UFW fell back on the boycott as its main weapon, as striking workers fanned out across the country to beef up boycott staffs.

The campaign to crush them took a heavy toll on the fledgling union. By the fall of 1973, the UFW held only a handful of the original 160 grape contracts it had won in 1970, and its membership fell to less than one-sixth of the 60,000 farm workers previously represented under UFW contracts.

Material support from the powerful trade union federation has been provided with an eyedropper. Meany and the other misleaders in the AFL-CIO have no desire to see a union of the type that the UFW is organizing because such a union poses a direct challenge to them. It is an example to the ranks of the AFL-CIO of the kind of trade union action necessary to defend and advance the interests of the working class today. Thus, the AFL-CIO officialdom has spent more time trying to pressure the UFW to shed its militant social approach to organizing farm workers in favor of the more "businesslike" ways of the AFL-CIO leadership than it has in aiding the embattled UFW. They have worked especially hard to get the UFW to adopt the AFL-CIO's scandalous stance in support of deportations.

The Chávez leadership has on occasion capitulated to this pressure. In the midst of the violent attacks on the UFW by growers and their Teamster collaborators in 1974, Chávez called for the deportation of Mexicano farm workers who were being used by the growers as strikebreaking scabs. The effect of Chávez's campaign was to focus attention on a section of the *campesinos* as a supposed obstacle in the way of a UFW victory, instead of aiming the union's fire at the growers, the government which supports them, and the collusion of the Teamster bureaucracy's thugs.

This scandalous error cost the union vital support among Chicanos and others and was unpopular in the ranks of the UFW. It cut into support for the union in the fields themselves, where Mexicanos with and without immigration visas look to the UFW as their voice. The prodeportation position of Chávez and other UFW leaders rapidly proved itself an obstacle to their goals. In the 1975 union representation elections provided for by the California Agricultural Labor Relations Act (ALRA), the growers and the Teamsters used immigration laws to deport hundreds of UFW supporters in an attempt to halt UFW victories in the elections.

Fortunately, this disastrous position of the UFW leadership was reversed at the union's 1975 convention, when the UFW announced that as long as the growers brought Mexicano workers into the fields to exploit them the UFW would organize them. In the elections in the fields they actively sought the support of undocumented workers; fought to defend them against *la migra,* the growers, and the Teamster officialdom's goons; and have won their support.

The passage of the ALRA in the summer of 1975 opened up a new stage in the UFW's efforts to organize farm labor. Against enormous odds in the elections, ranging from terror and intimidation tactics to outright fraud in the elections, the UFW out-polled the Teamsters two-to-one. These successes demonstrate the viability of *la causa* and indicate the deep roots that the UFW has among *campesinos.* The elections prove without a doubt that the UFW is the authentic voice of California's superexploited agricultural laborers.

The inspiration that *campesinos* throughout the United States have gained from the victories of the UFW in California has led to similar organizing efforts in Texas, Ohio, and parts of the East Coast. Although the UFW leadership has given little support to these efforts and tends to see them as detracting from the current drive in California, the UFW's continued existence in the face of powerful opposition, and its character as a social movement have provided the basic impulse to all these organizing efforts.

What agricultural workers need is one union that encompasses *all campesinos* on a national scale. Support to the UFW's boycott and organizing efforts, as well as other efforts of farm workers from Ohio to Texas and from Florida to New Jersey, can be a step to building such a united union.

The struggle in California's fields is far from over. The growers, and the capitalist parties that serve them, are out to crush the UFW, with help from the Teamster officialdom. They will concede nothing to the UFW without fighting every step of the way. California Democrats and Republicans have moved, on the growers' behalf, to nullify the hard-fought UFW victories in the union representation elections by cutting off funds for the Agricultural Labor Relations Board (ALRB), the body set up to conduct the elections and insure that the results are respected.

These maneuvers by the Democratic and Republican parties point to a central contradiction in the current UFW leadership. While the UFW's strength is the union's roots in the Chicano community and its appeal to the broad masses of American people as a social movement, the leadership's continued support to the Democratic Party that represents the growers' interests, not theirs, remains a glaring weakness of the UFW leaders. The illusion that California governor Edmund G. Brown, Jr., has the best interests of the UFW and the *campesinos* at heart is a deadly trap. The Democratic Party is tied hand and foot to agribusiness, not only in California, but nationally. Relying on this capitalist party is an obstacle to securing the gains the UFW won during its fifteen years of struggle and to registering further progress in the drive to organize the nation's three million agricultural workers.

In addition to strike actions in the fields, the UFW has utilized the boycott as a primary weapon. At the same time, its leaders have looked to "friendly" politicians, such as Brown, for help. Because they have placed so much confidence in these politicians, their ability to organize a broad and effective boycott and other mass actions is hampered. One example of this is the way the Chávez leadership responded to attacks by the California legislature on the farm labor law in spring 1976.

When the state legislature, with the collusion of California liberal Democrats, was strangling the bill to appropriate funds for the continued functioning of the ALRB, the UFW announced that it would put an initiative on the ballot to get California voters to pass such a bill. However, because UFW leaders were hoping that Brown and other leaders of the Democratic Party in California, who supposedly support the UFW, would get the proposition on the ballot for them, they postponed the petitioning drive week after week. Only when it became painfully clear that the UFW had been sold out by these "friends" in Sacramento did they begin petitioning to place the proposition on the ballot.

The UFW leadership's illusions in politicians like Brown hamper their ability to build a strong and effective boycott movement. Moreover, it leads the *campesinos* to place totally unjustified confidence in these capitalist politicians. Brown, who has tried to build his reputation in the national Democratic Party on the basis of his ability to bring "peace" to California's embattled fields, has continued to make speeches about his support to appropriations for the farm labor bill. At the same time, the Democratic speaker of the assembly, Leo McCarthy, has been actively working to throttle the ALRA. Now Brown has appointed McCarthy his campaign manager in his bid for the presidency. Chávez correctly attacks McCarthy for his role in trying to break the back of the farm labor bill, but has remained silent about Brown's intimate collaboration with McCarthy.

To the extent that the UFW leadership subordinates the mass action side of the UFW's struggle to reliance on "progressive" capitalist politicians like Brown, UFW victories in the fields and the effectiveness of the boycott will be undercut. A policy of class struggle in the fields and class collaboration in Sacramento can only be self-defeating.

The union must move to mobilize *in action* that huge reservoir of support and sympathy it has in the fields, in the Chicano community, on the campuses, within the trade unions, in the churches, and among other oppressed nationalities. Cutting loose from any policy of reliance on the Democratic Party and its politicians is a prerequisite for consciously developing and implementing such a perspective. Such a step would set a powerful example for the entire Chicano movement and would shake the current leadership of the trade union movement to its foundations.

The inspiration the UFW has already provided to the struggling masses would greatly increase, as would the chances for survival and progress of the United Farm Workers union itself.

Chicano Independent Political Action

These problems of political strategy and perspective are not restricted to the UFW. The same issues are posed for the entire labor movement and Chicano movement. The labor bureaucracy's long-standing policy of giving support to the political parties of the bosses and the resultant absence of any independent political voice of the working class is the central historic default of the American labor movement up to the present time.

The two-party system is the way the capitalist ruling class maintains its monopoly over the country's political life. The ruling rich own and control the Democratic and Republican parties, which are equally committed to preserving the capitalist system and its evils of war, racism, and exploitation. As one party begins to be discredited in the eyes of working people the other steps in for a while, pretending to offer something new. Then they trade back again. And so the runaround goes.

The illusion is deliberately fostered that the working class and the oppressed nationalities can win reforms and improve their condition by supporting their "friends" in these parties, or withholding support from their enemies. But reliance on either party facilitates the ruling class aim of diffusing and co-opting independent struggles of the masses, subordinating them to the needs of the capitalist system.

To advance its own goals the working class must break from the capitalist parties and steer a course of political independence. Its mass actions must be independent of these parties—not dependent on funds or favors from them, not concerned about embarrassing them, and not subordinated to getting them elected. Independent political action means putting nothing ahead of the demands and interests of the working class, the oppressed national minorities, women, and other victims of capitalism's degradation.

In order to break the two-party vise, the working class needs to form its own political party to give direction and reinforcement to its struggles and to pose the question of a different class governing society. A mass revolutionary workers' party is needed to lead the struggle to replace the capitalist rulers and establish a workers' government.

A giant step in this direction would be the formation of a labor party based on the organized power of the unions. This should not be a labor version of the Democratic and Republican parties or a vote-catching machine for up-and-coming "labor politicians." It should be a new type of party that strengthens the independent mobilization of all sectors of the oppressed and helps aim their force at the common enemy.

This strategic question of independent working class political action is posed with special acuteness for Chicanos, Blacks, and Puerto Ricans. These oppressed nationalities are overwhelmingly working class in composition. They have been victimized by many decades of concerted attempts by the ruling class to exclude them from the political life of this country. In the last decade and a half this has led to several attempts at the formation of independent Black or Chicano political parties. The growth of any such party would be a significant step forward in winning the democratic rights of Chicano or Black political representation. It would also be a big step toward breaking with the political parties of the oppressors and charting a course of independent working class political action. The Raza Unida parties that have grown out of Chicano struggles are the most advanced expression of this kind to be found in the United States today.

The native Mexican inhabitants of the Southwest were forcibly and violently displaced from the land they once owned by the expansion and consolidation of U.S. capitalism. In the crucible of ascending American imperialism a distinct oppressed nationality was forged. This process entailed the systematic denial of political rights to the second class Chicano citizens of the Southwest. In part this was accomplished by the open use of terror. Like Blacks in the South, Chicanos knew that attempts to utilize their political rights could cost them their lives or livelihoods.

The victories of the Black civil rights struggles brought some changes for Chicanos too. However, even with the enforcement of formal political guarantees, the use of English as the only legal political language served to effectively prevent Chicanos from exercising their rights and restricted their participation in the political life of the country.

This fact was finally recognized even by the U.S. Congress in 1975 when the 1965 Voting Rights Act was extended for another ten years and broadened by making bilingual elections mandatory in districts where more than 5 percent of the voters do not speak English.

The fight of Chicanos for political representation has generated numerous struggles over the years. However, until very recently virtually all attempts at political activity have been channeled through the Democratic Party. For example, organizations like the Mexican-American Political Association (MAPA) in California and the Political Association of Spanish-speaking Organizations (PASO) in Texas were established in the late 1950s for the purpose of pressing the Democratic Party into addressing itself to the needs of Chicanos. MAPA and PASO register Chicanos to vote, organize the Chicano vote for the Democrats, and seek to get Chicano Democrats elected to public office. Those Chicanos who go to the polls vote in their great majority for the Democratic Party.

While there has been a slight increase in the number of Chicanos elected to office, Chicanos are still miserably underrepresented on all governmental levels. An example is Los Angeles County, where well over one million Chicanos reside. The first Chicano congressperson from this area was elected in 1962, 112 years after California gained statehood. There is no Chicano representation on the fifteen-member Los Angeles city council, and no Chicano has ever been elected to the powerful five-member L.A. County Board of Supervisors. This latter body administers East Los Angeles, the largest Chicano barrio in the country. In three special elections the Democratic Party machine in Los Angeles County has successfully stymied efforts to incorporate the area into a separate city.

Over the last decade, faced with rising Chicano militancy, the Democratic Party has stepped up its efforts to hold on to the Chicano vote. One reflection of this was the election in 1974 of two Chicano governors—for the first time in history. The fact that there has been an increase, however slight, of Chicano elected officials in the last decade is a token of the deepening nationalist consciousness among Chicanos and an expression of their desires to be represented in the political arena by their own people.

However, the election of Chicano Democrats does not represent a form of independent political action. On the contrary, it is a way of perpetuating Chicano *dependence* on those who are responsible for the second class status of Chicanos and other oppressed sectors of the population.

Toward the end of the 1960s, deepening disillusionment with the Democratic Party led a layer of Chicano militants to break from the perspective of working inside this party and move toward organizing independent political formations. The concept of independent Chicano political action was first discussed and debated on a national scale at the National Chicano Youth Liberation conferences held in 1969 and 1970 in Denver,

Colorado. The conferences were called by the Denver Crusade for Justice, an urban civil rights and Chicano cultural organization that emerged in the mid-1960s. The Crusade's central leader, Rodolfo "Corky" Gonzales, had been a Democratic Party functionary in Denver, but broke from the Democrats when he became convinced that such a party was incapable of responding to or fighting for the needs of Chicanos.

It was in the wake of the struggles of the 1960s and following these discussions and debates that the Raza Unida parties emerged, representing the most sustained attempts yet to develop Chicano political action. The Raza Unida parties also represent a step toward independent political action by the working class as a whole.

In order to have a real voice in American politics, the Chicano people need a *mass* party, organizationally and politically independent of the twin parties of capitalist rule. The kind of party Chicanos need would confront the capitalist class in the electoral arena by posing a nationalist and class alternative for Chicanos at the polls. But it would not only be an electoral tool. It could also mobilize and lead the Chicano masses in actions in the streets in order to press for their day-to-day needs—such as more and better jobs, decent housing, bilingual and bicultural education, a halt to racist deportations. Such a party, basing itself on a program and perspective of class-struggle action, could open the way for new alignments and alliances with other oppressed and exploited groups and prove an effective means of promoting and protecting the interests of Chicanos in the social, economic, and political arenas.

The development of such a mass independent Chicano political party would have a profound impact on American politics. It would, in fact, herald the doom of the capitalist two-party system. The Democrats rely heavily on votes from a combination of labor and the oppressed national minorities. If Chicanos were to turn away from the Democratic Party on a massive scale, it would significantly weaken the Democrats, particularly in the Southwest, where the Chicano vote is essential for Democratic Party victories. Unable to win, the Democratic Party coalition would shatter. The example set by a mass independent Chicano political party would be an inspiring lesson to Blacks, Puerto Ricans, and other working people, and encourage the development of independent political action on the part of labor and the Black and Puerto Rican communities.

A mass political party of this type does not yet exist. The various Raza Unida Party formations and the successes they have chalked up in their six years of existence have helped to deepen the understanding among Chicanos and others of the need to break from the Democratic Party. But while these parties are the most advanced forms of political organization yet to emerge in the Chicano struggle, their development has been limited and uneven. To understand some of the problems these small parties face, it is useful to look at the development of the Raza Unida parties in California, Colorado, and Texas.

California

The clearest example of the unevenness of the Raza Unida parties is the limited development and growth of the California parties, particularly the Raza Unida groupings in Los Angeles.

For the most part, parties in Fresno, San Diego, San José and Oakland exist only as paper organizations or as very small groupings. In general, the parties in these areas have not utilized the openings provided by elections to build a strong base among Chicanos, nor have they participated as parties in the concrete struggles of Chicanos in their areas.

An example of this is the Oakland Raza Unida Party, which had a promising start in 1971-72. It elaborated a program which was an example for other Raza Unida parties to emulate and ran a Raza Unida Party slate in the 1971 elections. Through this and other activities, it won important support among Chicanos in the Oakland–San Francisco Bay Area.

The leaders of this Raza Unida formation came out of a militant struggle by Chicano and Latino students at Merritt College, a community college in Oakland. The student struggles won the establishment of Chicano and Latin American studies departments, as well as other programs for Chicano and Latino students. But after a successful start the Oakland Raza Unida Party leaders bent to the pressure of ultraleft and sectarian activists who were opposed to any participation in electoral activity with its implicit orientation to organizing the Chicano masses. The perspective of building an independent Chicano political party was abandoned.

In Los Angeles, the large size of the Chicano population opens broad opportunities for the construction of a powerful and effective independent Chicano political party. Such a development would have a profound impact on politics in that city, as well as the country as a whole. It could win significant support from Blacks and unionists—initially among Chicano unionists in particular who are active in the Chicano movement.

Despite this potential, the various Raza Unida Party groupings in Los Angeles are small and divided. In several local election campaigns run by Raza Unida Party groupings in Los Angeles, significant support was registered. The response to the RUP campaigns of Raul Ruiz for state assembly against a Chicano Democrat in 1972, and for city council in the special election for incorporation of East Los Angeles in 1974, indicated the sentiment among Chicanos for a party truly representing their interests in the political arena. Had East Los Angeles been incorporated into a separate city, it would have been the largest Chicano city in the country and Raul Ruiz, who outpolled Democrats in the race, would have been on the first city council.

Another indication of the sentiment for an independent Chicano party in Los Angeles is the development of the San Fernando Valley chapter of the Raza Unida Party. While the group is small, it has deep roots in the Chicano community of the valley and has carried out consistent activity in defense of Chicano rights on the job, in the schools, and other struggles in the community. It has also fielded candidates in local elections.

However, despite the extensive pro–Raza Unida Party sentiment that has already been demonstrated in California, no leadership has yet emerged that has been able to consolidate that support and start to build a mass party that organizes Chicanos to fight for their needs, using every avenue available.

Colorado

In Colorado, the Raza Unida Party was initiated and led by the Denver Crusade for Justice. The RUP in Denver was established in 1970, about the same time the party in Crystal City, Texas, was formed. The militant leaders of the Crusade, especially Corky Gonzáles, demonstrated the clearest understanding of the need for Chicano political action independent of the Democratic Party. They ran Chicano candidates against the Democrats and Republicans in local elections in 1970, and through this the concept of an independent Chicano political party got a broad hearing among Chicanos for the first time in Denver.

In the initial stages of its formation, the Colorado Raza Unida Party showed the greatest promise of developing into an important component of the future mass independent Chicano political party. Gonzales and other Crusade leaders saw the need for this important question to be discussed and debated broadly in the Chicano movement on a national scale. The national Chicano Youth Liberation conferences in 1969, 1970, and 1971 in Denver provided an arena for rich discussion on the strategy of independent Chicano political action. Thousands of Chicanos from across the country participated.

The main base of the Colorado Raza Unida Party has always been in Denver, where the Crusade for Justice has had deep roots in the Chicano community. But by participating as an independent formation in statewide and county elections in 1972 and 1974, the party was able to extend its influence into southern Colorado, and established functioning chapters in Weld County and Pueblo, where there are sizable Chicano populations.

A weakness of the Colorado Raza Unida Party is that it has always been projected as the electoral instrument of the Crusade. This is an obstacle to winning large numbers of Chicanos to the Raza Unida banner because few are ready to make the kind of commitment of time and energy that the cadres of the Crusade make. Moreover, the Raza Unida Party does not participate as a party in the daily struggles of Chicanos in Denver and throughout the state. To the extent that activity around concrete demands being pressed by the Chicano community takes place, this is carried out by the Crusade. Thus the Raza Unida Party itself does not take the lead in organizing Chicanos in Denver to counter the racist offensive against bilingual-bicultural education, to fight for jobs for Chicanos who are being hit hard with discriminatory layoffs, or to demand solutions to the many other problems confronting Chicanos today.

Differences over perspectives for building the Colorado Raza Unida Party and assuring its democratic functioning led to the disbanding of the Greeley Raza Unida grouping, the backbone of the Weld County RUP. Some of its key leaders have since become Maoists.

All of these political problems are exacerbated by the government repression that has come down hard on the Crusade in the last few years. The government's stepped-up attacks began with the 1973 police assault on the Crusade's school, Escuela Tlatelolco, in which one Chicano youth was murdered by the cops, and scores of others arrested on frame-up charges designed to make the victims into the criminals in the eyes of the public.

Since 1973, a systematic campaign of harassment and intimidation has been carried out, forcing the Crusade and Raza Unida Party leaders to expend considerable time and resources fighting legal frame-ups ranging from traffic violations to bombing charges. The killings of six Raza Unida Party student activists in two 1974 bombing incidents in Boulder dramatized the murderous character of the government's terror campaign.

The latest outrage was the arrest of Juan Haro in the fall of 1975. A key leader of the Raza Unida Party and cofounder of the Crusade for Justice, Haro was framed up, along with a young Crusade activist, on charges of conspiring to bomb a Denver police substation. The chief witness for the prosecution in the case was an informer and provocateur hired by the Alcohol, Tobacco and Firearms Bureau of the Treasury Department to infiltrate the Crusade.* The direct complicity of the federal government in the conspiracy to discredit, isolate, and, if possible, destroy the Crusade and the Raza Unida Party in Denver is clear. The Chicano movement and its supporters must organize to force the government to open its files in order to uncover the truth about the victimization of the Crusade and other operations the capitalist government is carrying out to destroy the Chicano movement, or frame up its militants.

The attack on the Crusade and the Colorado Raza Unida Party is an attack on the entire Chicano movement. A mobilization of the Chicano community and its allies in defense of the Crusade is needed to force the government to halt the murderous drive against this Chicano organization.

An initiative by the Crusade to launch a broad defense committee open to all who want to help them fight back, regardless of political differences on other questions, would be a powerful rejoinder to the government's attempts to isolate and destroy them.

Texas

The survival of the Texas party, growing support for it throughout the state, and its accomplishments over the last six years offer the best testimony to the viability of the concept of an independent Chicano political party.

The Texas party emerged out of a militant Chicano student struggle led by MAYO in the small South Texas town of Crystal

---

*Juan Haro was acquitted of all charges connected with the bomb plot in April 1977.

City. Crystal City is overwhelmingly Chicano, and the 1969 struggle by Chicano high school students protesting racist practices in their schools sparked a mobilization in the Chicano community and a fight to gain control over the schools in the town. The community organization set up to support the blowouts, Ciudadanos Unidos (United Citizens), formed the basic core of the Raza Unida Party, along with MAYO. Independent candidates were fielded for school board in 1970 and they won. The impact of the 1970 electoral victories inspired the growth of Raza Unida parties all over South Texas. In many towns, Chicanos comprise a majority of the population.

Since then, the Raza Unida parties have won elections for school board, city council, justice of the peace, mayor, and other city and county offices in a number of small South Texas towns.

Programmatically, these parties aspire to Chicano control of institutions in the Chicano community. In Crystal City, for example, the Raza Unida Party holds a majority of seats on the school board, city council, and several positions in Zavala County, of which Crystal City is the seat. In 1974, José Angel Gutiérrez, a founder of the Crystal City RUP, was elected to a Zavala County judgeship. The Raza Unida Party-run Crystal City administration has instituted bilingual-bicultural programs and free school lunches, and hired Chicanos to replace racist teachers in Crystal City schools. When the Raza Unida Party candidates took office one of their first actions was to demand that the hated Texas Rangers get out of Crystal City and stay out. They recently waged a court battle against the major utility company that services Crystal City in an effort to halt a hike in gas and electric rates.

The Raza Unida city administration also aided Chicano workers in the Del Monte cannery—the major business in Crystal City—to set up their own union, Obreros Unidos Independientes (United Independent Workers), because the Teamsters local that supposedly represented them signed a contract with the boss behind the cannery workers' backs.

Important as these gains have been, they also point up the severe limitations on what can be accomplished through gaining control of the city administration and schools in one or two towns, particularly small towns like Crystal City.

A limited amount can be changed through Raza Unida administration of city governments, especially those, like Crystal City, lacking in the financial resources necessary to institute meaningful changes in the lives of Chicanos. Crystal City itself is impoverished, as are most of the small towns in South Texas. The main power and wealth is in the hands of a few Anglo ranchers in Zavala County.

In order to significantly improve the depressed living conditions of Chicanos, Raza Unida Party city and county administrations have to rely on state and federal funds. To insure that these state and federal programs are tailored to the demands of Chicanos and administered by them, it is necessary to organize and mobilize the Chicano community to fight to force government financing of schools, jobs, housing, health care, child care, and other social programs necessary to improve the lot of Chicanos. To be effective, such a struggle has to be carried out on a scale beyond the local area and has to involve Chicanos and their allies across the Southwest to secure these gains.

However, many of the key leaders of the Texas Raza Unida Party have tended toward a one-sided view of what the Raza Unida Party can be. They limit their strategy to building viable chapters of the RUPs in those South Texas counties where Chicanos are a majority and can win electoral victories with the goal of becoming the local and county administration.

Raza Unida Party statewide electoral campaigns in 1972 and 1974 departed from this strategy and pointed the way forward in building the influence and mass base of the independent Chicano political party among the masses of Chicanos throughout Texas. These campaigns extended the Raza Unida parties into major urban centers where Chicanos represent a significant minority. They led to the establishment of Raza Unida Party chapters in Houston, Dallas, Fort Worth, San Antonio, El Paso, and Corpus Christi. These statewide RUP campaigns also began to win a hearing among some Black and labor organizations, and helped to popularize the concept of independent Chicano political action on a broad scale.

However, the Texas Raza Unida Party is still seen by some of its leaders and activists as simply an electoral party—a vote-winning machine. As a result, the Chicano political formations have tended to function as political parties only during elections. The RUP is not yet being built as a political party, organized on a year-round basis and doing more than running candidates in elections.

Because of the monopoly the Democratic and Republican

parties have over the political life of the country, the American masses identify politics with elections, and view political parties as electoral machines. This concept is consciously perpetuated by the capitalist class.

The Chicano masses will look to the Raza Unida parties as *their* party only when they see these parties can lead them in their daily struggles. This will aid in deepening the consciousness among Chicanos of the need for more fundamental social change to end the racist oppression they suffer, and to seek allies that can help accomplish this.

Such an approach would mean that after the vote is in, time is spent in consolidating the support registered at the polls by projecting consistent activity to involve supporters of the Raza Unida Party. Mass activities carried out would be organized and led by the RUPs during elections and also when there is no election on the agenda. Currently, most of such activities involving RUP supporters are organized by Ciudadanos Unidos or Familias Unidas and other groups in Texas. Thus, outside of Zavala County, the Raza Unida Party has no public face between elections. To one degree or another, all the RUPs have had this same limitation.

The Raza Unida parties are trying to grapple with a very fundamental problem. How do you get from the initiating core of activists who are already convinced of the need to break from capitalist parties to a party that has the allegiance and active participation of the Chicano masses? How do you, at the same time, put forward and fight around a program of immediate, democratic, and transitional demands that can propel Chicanos into action against their oppression at all levels and attract growing numbers of allies?

There is no contradiction between putting forward a program of clear demands around the social, political, and economic oppression of Chicanos and winning the Chicano masses to the banners of the Raza Unida parties. To the contrary, the only way to build a powerful Chicano movement and a mass independent Chicano political party is precisely through fighting uncompromisingly around concrete demands that move Chicanos in the direction of mass anticapitalist mobilization, advancing them toward the goal of their liberation. Such actions also have the potential of forcing meaningful concessions from the government. Without projecting themselves as such a movement, the Raza Unida parties run the risk of losing their independent thrust or making errors that can isolate them from the masses of Chicanos.

The problem of political perspective in the Raza Unida parties was most clearly expressed in the months leading up to the 1972 National Raza Unida Parties convention held in El Paso, Texas. Prior to the convention, some RUP leaders argued for adoption of a strategy that could have transformed the RUPs into nothing more than a pressure group seeking concessions from the Democratic and Republican parties.

Differences over this strategy were never openly debated on the floor of the El Paso convention and remain unclarified. But the overwhelming majority of delegates at that convention took a stand reaffirming the independence of the Raza Unida parties from the two parties of capitalist rule. They refused to endorse either George McGovern or Richard Nixon in their presidential bids. This was an important test of viability which these parties passed.

While no one in the leadership of the Raza Unida parties is today arguing for a "pressure group" perspective and, in fact, the RUPs continue to remain independent from the Democratic and Republican parties, the danger still remains that these relatively small Chicano parties will find the increasing pressure from the capitalist parties overwhelming.

At the present time there is no organized wing or leading figure within the RUPs consciously attempting to bring these parties back into the Democratic Party. But until these parties develop a clear program of demands aimed at mobilizing the Chicanos *in action* to fight for their needs and aspirations, and until they go beyond an electoral perspective, there remains the danger of a drift back into the Democratic Party.

Another problem is related to this one. Many of the activists and leaders of the Raza Unida parties understand that Chicanos are a minority in American society and see the need to win allies to their struggles in order to register gains, not only in the electoral arena, but in the schools, the courts, the factories and workplaces, the unions, and elsewhere.

This was reflected in the 1974 Raza Unida gubernatorial campaign of Ramsey Muñiz in Texas. Muñiz and other Texas leaders looked to Blacks, labor, and others as natural allies for their campaign and tried to win support among these layers of the population. This was a very positive sentiment. However, some RUP activists and leaders thought that they could win these allies to support of the RUP campaign by ducking the question of the Chicano composition of the Raza Unida parties and by watering down the nationalist and class demands put forward in the past in response to Chicanos' needs. When he spoke to Anglo audiences, for example, Muñiz defined the Raza Unida Party as "United People's Party." Though this did not result in winning any significant Anglo support for the campaign, it served to confuse activists who have joined the Raza Unida Party or support it because they see it as the voice of *Chicanos* in the political arena.

Any Chicano party that addresses itself to the issues affecting Chicanos today will find it necessary, first and most of all, to elaborate a program of economic and social demands to win gains for Chicanos. Such a program will likewise be attractive to and win support from other working people and oppressed layers of the population who have the same problems. The Raza Unida parties are correct in appealing to allies of the Chicano people, but these allies are going to be won only if the RUP is able to rally some significant Chicano support to its banner.

The question of winning allies for the Chicano struggle is inseparable from the question of how to win the majority of Chicanos away from their capitalist exploiters in the political arena, and to a party that is not only their tribune in the elections, but leads Chicanos in struggle 365 days out of the year. There is no shortcut to *politically* winning the Chicano people to the banners of the RUPs. To do this, it is necessary to combine electoral activity with mass action in the streets. Moreover, the Raza Unida parties will have to actively involve their members in determining the direction and policies of the party. While organizations such as Ciudadanos Unidos and Familias Unidas in Texas, and the Crusade for Justice in Denver are valuable and important tools for winning support for the Raza Unida parties, they cannot substitute for broad participation in the decision-making process within the Raza Unida parties.

The Socialist Workers Party

The Socialist Workers Party will continue to do everything possible to support the building of the Raza Unida parties as independent Chicano political organizations capable of advancing the Chicano liberation struggle. Not only does this mean giving active support to Raza Unida candidates who are clearly running independent from the capitalist parties, where appropriate; it means contributing our ideas and suggestions and participating in the discussion within the Chicano movement over all aspects of program and perspectives. It means helping to build the actions that can mobilize Chicanos in struggle—by the farm workers, steelworkers, women, students, antideportation forces, supporters of affirmative action.

It means presenting our revolutionary socialist ideas and perspectives through the election campaigns of the Socialist Workers Party, through the pages of the *Militant,* through *Intercontinental Press,* the bilingual weekly magazine of the Fourth International, through sales of the press of the Mexican Trotskyists, and through all our various activities.

In the early stages of the resurgence of Chicano nationalism, those who held that only a socialist revolution would bring about the total liberation of the Chicano people were a very small minority in the Chicano movement. Chicano revolutionary socialists often were forced to fight for their right to participate in Chicano movement organizations, and the right to present their ideas in discussions of Chicano movement perspectives. A large majority of Chicano militants, who were new to radical politics, believed that revolutionary theories in general, and Marxism and Leninism in particular, were at best irrelevant to the struggle. Some Chicano leaders argued heatedly that Marxist ideas were in fact dangerous to Chicanos because they were "Anglo theories."

However, a significant change has begun to take place in the last several years. There is widespread interest in socialist ideas, history, and perspectives among a growing number of Chicanos. At virtually every Chicano gathering in the last two years, there have been lively debates on the relevance of socialism to the struggles of Chicanos. Chicano militants, especially youth, are reading more revolutionary literature than at any time in the past. Increasing numbers of Chicano studies departments carry courses on Marxism and Chicano liberation, and invite socialists to address these and other classes. The newspapers and magazines of the Chicano movement carry more articles on socialism and the Chicano movement. Marxist study groups have been set up by some Chicano organizations, and many Chicanos participate in others. Socialist candidates and spokespeople are getting a broader hearing in the Chicano movement.

The discussions and debates that are going on within the Chicano movement pose new challenges and opportunities for the

Socialist Workers Party. Chicano militants are weighing the merits of all the tendencies in the workers' movement and are scrutinizing their programs and positions. The SWP has more opportunities than at any time in its history to present its program for socialism to Chicanos and win growing numbers of Chicanos to its ranks. It must be prepared to provide the answers and the education that Chicanos are seeking, not only on Chicano nationalism, but also on economic theory, and the whole range of Marxism that is the foundation of the SWP's program.

The SWP unconditionally supports the Chicano struggle for self-determination. It believes that the development of Chicano nationalism is a positive step forward in the struggle for Chicano liberation. The SWP recognizes that the struggle of Chicanos against their oppression takes place on two intertwined fronts—a fight against the oppression they face as a people, and a struggle against their exploitation as part of the working class. Only the coming American socialist revolution—a proletarian revolution that also completes the unfulfilled democratic tasks of the bourgeois revolution by assuring equality and self-determination to the oppressed national minorities in the United States—can bring about the total liberation of Chicanos.

Understanding this combined character of the coming American revolution differentiates the SWP from every other tendency in the workers' movement—the Stalinist Communist Party and Maoist sects, the social democrats, the sectarian leftists. The Socialist Workers Party's aim is to construct a mass revolutionary Leninist party that aspires to lead the working class and its allies to power to achieve both of these goals. The American working class has the momentous task of wresting state power from the most powerful ruling class on earth. The necessity of carrying out such a transformation is becoming clearer and clearer as the breakdowns and crises of the capitalist system spread. But to accomplish this task the working class will need something it does not yet have—its own mass revolutionary socialist party.

We are confident that explosive events will promote rapid changes in the political consciousness of the working class and lead to upsurges out of which a mass revolutionary socialist party can emerge. However, this can happen only if the cadres of this party are assembled beforehand around a clear perspective and program. This is what the Socialist Workers Party is doing.

Only a party that is deeply rooted in the working class, especially among its most oppressed sectors, can lead the American working class and its allies to power. This involves systematic work in all sectors of the mass movement to recruit the most capable fighters to the revolutionary party. There is no way that the working class can achieve its aims unless it brings together in a common fighting party and develops into revolutionary cadres the most resolute revolutionists of the working class and the best fighters from all the oppressed national minorities—Black, Chicano, Puerto Rican, Native American, and Asian-American.

As the nucleus of the future mass revolutionary socialist party, the SWP puts forward a program and perspective of struggle that can help mobilize Chicanos and all working people to fight for their interests. The working class cannot achieve its goals without the Chicano people and other nationally oppressed peoples achieving theirs.

The deepening contradictions of U.S. imperialism and the heavy burden this will place on the Chicano population will generate increased struggles in the period ahead. The SWP must be part of these struggles, rooting itself more deeply in the Chicano masses.

The SWP's task is to win more Chicanos to the revolutionary socialist party and educate them as revolutionary cadres. The steps taken to establish new SWP units in San José, San Antonio, East Los Angeles, the Mission District of San Francisco, and other cities help facilitate the party's work in organizing itself to meet new openings. The SWP's ability to win increasing numbers of Chicano revolutionists will be a fundamental test of our capacities as a revolutionary party.

Chicano Liberation Report to the 1976 SWP Convention

This report was given by Olga Rodríguez to the August 1976 SWP convention.

The National Committee resolution on the Chicano struggle ["The Crisis of American Capitalism and the Struggle for Chicano Liberation"] states:

"Despite any temporary upturns, American capitalism has entered a long-term period of economic crisis and stagnation. The future will generally see higher, not lower, unemployment levels; high inflation rates; fewer, not more, social services; falling, not rising, standards of living for working people.

"In keeping with a centuries-old policy of divide and rule, the American ruling class will make every effort to shift a disproportionate burden of this economic crisis onto the Chicano population."

A recent issue of the Spanish-language weekly *El Sol de Texas* offered a striking illustration of how Chicanos have fared under more than 100 years of American capitalist rule. While the bands struck up "The Yankee Doodle Boy" on the 200th birthday of the Declaration of Independence, health officials in New Mexico were treating Chicanos for bubonic plague. In another part of Aztlán—the Rio Grande Valley of Texas—a local television station aired a program last fall on the increased number of cases of leprosy in the "magic valley," as the wealthy gringo ranchers call the area.

A common feature in these isolated regions of the Southwest that contributes to the thriving of diseases generally associated with the Dark Ages, or the most impoverished countries in the semicolonial world, is the absence of an adequate sanitation system. In many of the *colonias* of the valley, for example, running water is a rare service.

Infant mortality among Chicano migrant workers in these areas remains 125 percent higher than the national average, and the incidence of tuberculosis and other infectious diseases is 250 percent higher than in the rest of the country.

Chicanos in the barrios of major cities throughout the Southwest—where the bulk of the Chicano population lives— have not fared much better. Nearly one-third of the Chicano population in Aztlán occupy deteriorating and dilapidated housing.

These chronic problems plaguing the Chicano people are getting worse. The much-touted recovery of the economy has meant little to Chicanos. Nearly 13 percent of the Chicano work force was unemployed in March 1975. The jobless rate for Chicanos today remains nearly double the national average. In cities such as Los Angeles, Chicano unemployment is estimated by some to be as high as 45 percent, and for Chicano youth, a staggering 60 percent.

Chicanos had made some important economic and social strides forward in the late 1960s. But the effects of the last five years of economic crisis laid to rest the idea that the gap that separates the standards of living of Chicanos and whites could even be significantly narrowed, much less closed. The latest data available show that in 1974 the average Chicano family had an income of $9,498. That's 74 percent of the income of $12,836 for the average family. More than one-third of all Chicano families live below the federal government's poverty line. The income gap between Chicano and Anglo wages can be expected to widen.

Chicanos have been among the first victims of the government's drive to roll back social gains. From the massive assault on social services, to the racist offensive abetted by the government at all levels, Chicano rights to equal education, decent housing, and jobs are being challenged.

Immigration and Deportations

A major component of this attack is the virulently racist campaign against Mexicanos and others living and working in the United States without immigration visas or work permits— the so-called illegal aliens.

The importance of this issue is underscored by the recent escalation of immigration raids and deportations in San Antonio. As the social and economic crisis of U.S. imperialism deepens, this issue will be driven to the fore. The conditions that compel Mexicanos and others to brave crossing the U.S. border without papers will become more severe in the period ahead.

Last April, the *New York Times* reported on a speech by Benjamin Holman, then director of the Community Relations Service, an agency of the U.S. Justice Department. Holman said that the present Latino population in the United States is fast approaching the 20 million mark. This figure represents those "citizen" Latinos whom the government counts, and the undocumented, or "illegal," Latinos in the United States. This "brown tide" is "an evolving internal problem with both national and international consequences," according to Holman.

The 1975 census update put the Latino population at 11.2 million—an increase of more than 1 million since 1970. The Immigration and Naturalization Service—*la migra*—estimates that there are more than 8 million workers from Latin America without immigration papers in the country today. Of these, 90 percent are Mexicanos. Sixty percent of us "legal" Latinos counted by the U.S. Census Bureau are Chicanos.

It is clear even from these distorted government studies that the Chicano population is growing. The question of further and more significant growth is posed by the massive Mexican immigration during the last decade.

In the first half of the twentieth century, Mexican immigration played a major role in boosting the size and social weight of the Chicano nationality. The Mexicanos who migrated then were quickly forced into the mold of oppression cast by American capitalist expansion in the Southwest in 1848.

While current immigration from Mexico needs closer study, it is safe to say that it is by far the most massive immigration ever from Mexico. Some important parallels and differences with earlier waves can be noted:

1. Mass immigration from Mexico in the past occurred during periods of deep social and economic upheaval—such as during and following the Mexican revolution which began in 1910, the worldwide depression of the 1930s, and during World War II. Semicolonial conditions in Mexico spurred immigration to the United States.

2. This immigration was encouraged by U.S. capitalism in the first half of the twentieth century. American capitalists were quick to recognize that the impoverished Mexicanos provide a highly exploitable, inexpensive labor pool. This was true particularly for the rapidly expanding agribusiness in the Southwest.

3. The basic pattern of Mexicano immigration had been from the rural areas in Mexico to the border towns in the Southwest.

Unlike their predecessors, the new Mexican immigrants tend to move directly to major cities in the Southwest and Midwest in hopes of finding jobs in industry. For example, it is estimated that the Latino population in the Chicago-Great Lakes area now exceeds that of New Mexico, Arizona, and Colorado combined. While this includes Puertorriqueños and other Latinos, most of these new immigrants are from Mexico.

The capitalists complain about the differences between Mexicanos coming to the United States today and those who came in previous immigration waves. As one cop in San Antonio put it: "They are younger and younger and more and more are from the cities, rather than the rural areas, especially those from Mexico. For this reason," he added in dismay, "they are better able to blend into the city's culture, making them a lot harder to detect."

The tempo at which these Mexicano immigrants will be absorbed into the Chicano nationality is something that we cannot determine. But as the crisis deepens, the capitalist rulers will proceed to roll back the social gains the American working class and its allies won over decades of class struggle. In the process the hysteria against *all* "foreign" workers—including Chicanos—will continue to be whipped up to a fever pitch.

The question of Mexican immigration is increasingly urgent for the Chicano movement. In addition to massive deportations, the government is on a campaign to wipe out bilingual programs. Of the 20 million Latinos estimated to be in the United States today, more than 80 percent view Spanish as their first language, according to government statisticians. Instead of expanding bilingual programs the government is cutting back the few such programs that exist. The capitalists are trying to ram legislation through to curtail the rights of Chicanos, as well as Mexicanos and other Latinos with and without papers. They will try to make the "illegal aliens" the scapegoats for more of the nation's economic and social woes—from rising unemployment to the increase in crime and disease. No one should be surprised if

Pennsylvania health officials announce that the cause of the mysterious deaths in Philadelphia among patriotic American Legionnaires was the presence of "illegal aliens" working as waiters!

The U.S. Supreme Court recently upheld the INS's right to establish immigration checkpoints near the Mexican border, and its right to stop all those suspected of being "illegal aliens." The high court's decision reversed an earlier ruling by a San Francisco court to close such checkpoints, because they constituted a violation of the Fourth Amendment protection against unreasonable search and seizure.

The Border Patrol checkpoints are a frightening and degrading experience for any Chicano or Mexicano. We are the ones stopped and shaken down as "suspected illegals" because we are brown. The Supreme Court's decision strikes another blow to the democratic rights of Chicanos and all working people to travel freely without harassment.

The capitalists will continue to counterpose jobs to full democratic and civil rights for all who live and work in this country. The narrow-minded, racist labor bureaucracy is an enthusiastic advocate of the government's drive against undocumented workers, helping to embolden *la migra*.

Both San Antonio daily newspapers ran *the same* anti-Mexicano series to alert the public to what they portrayed as disease-ridden, job-stealing criminals pouring across the border. The local affiliate of a major network featured three-minute editorial spots every night for several nights, warning of the "alien invasion." From what people in San Antonio tell me, the television spots were aired with as much drama as if there were indeed an invasion from outer space.

The kind of hysteria that is being whipped up against Mexicanos without papers has the ring of the xenophobic campaign that was carried out during the 1940s. That drive led to a week of vicious attacks by rampaging Anglo servicemen on Chicanos and Mexicanos in Los Angeles in the so-called Pachuco, or Zoot Suit, Riots. Only it's a little different today. Chicanos are less willing to tolerate such blatant racist attacks.

In addition to these deportations, the government is attempting to silence all opposition to its racist drive. The arrests last month of two Chicano movement leaders in San Antonio illustrate this. Ignacio "Nacho" Pérez, a leader of the San Antonio Raza Unida Party and former leader of MAYO [Mexican-American Youth

Organization], was indicted on charges of "shielding illegal aliens from detection." Mario Cantú, the other victim of the government's frame-up, was arrested last month by U.S. marshals on a charge of conspiracy to "harbor illegal aliens." Cantú, a well-known activist in the antideportation movement and longtime leader of the Chicano movement in San Antonio, committed the "crime" of demanding that immigration authorities produce a search warrant before raiding his restaurant.

In a city that is majority Chicano and Mexicano, it's not easy for the capitalists to convince Chicanos that massive dragnet raids to hunt out undocumented Mexicanos in the barrios, at churches, at funerals and weddings, and on the job are in their interest as Chicanos!

Of course, the government tries. The capitalists use the media they control to convince Chicanos, who suffer high unemployment in San Antonio and elsewhere, that Mexicanos are stealing jobs that rightfully belong to Chicanos. But more and more Chicanos are rejecting this lie. They don't accept that the only way they can have a job is to deny human and civil rights to their Mexican brothers and sisters who happen to lack work visas. The government is then forced to fall back on methods of intimidation and violence to convince Chicanos and everyone else that they will pay a price if they fight for the rights of undocumented Raza workers.

The arrests of Cantú and Pérez have already begun to generate an angry response from Chicanos and others in San Antonio.

The main task before the Chicano movement today is to mount a counteroffensive to this and other assaults on the rights and living standards of Chicanos. Unfortunately, the Chicano movement and its allies have lacked an organized and united response to the government campaign. Let's take a look at where those forces that have mobilized in the past in defense of undocumented workers stand today.

CASA (Centro de Acción Social Autónomo) grew out of the struggles of Chicanos in 1968 in response to deportation of Mexicanos. The organization was founded in Los Angeles by Bert Corona and is still looked on by most activists in the Chicano movement as the main antideportation organization. CASA, however, no longer sees itself as an organization that fights solely for the rights of undocumented workers. Its present leadership in Los Angeles has turned instead in a sectarian and workerist direction.

While CASA maintains that the issue of deportations is an important one facing working people, it has taken a step away from mobilizing mass actions in defense of Mexicanos and others without papers. The Los Angeles leadership of CASA, which basically sets policy for CASA supporters elsewhere, now defines CASA as a mass revolutionary workers' organization. They stated in a special magazine they passed out to participants at the National Chicano Forum in Salt Lake City:

". . . in summing up our experiences of the last decade and putting these experiences in the proper historical context of the Mexican workers' involvement in class struggles both here and south of the border we come to the conclusion that we must: organize the unorganized, unite with honest forces committed to building Socialism, forge a unity for the historical task at hand, and be prepared to wage principled struggle for the unity of our people and our class."

Their only proposal for how to respond to massive deportations is contained in the "Call" in the same publication. They write:

"We call for the united resistance of the Mexican people. We must refuse to produce any documents in response to the racist demands of the immigration agents."

While such sentiments of solidarity are admirable, they are hardly the way the mass of Chicanos and other working people— who are confused on the question of undocumented workers—can be convinced of the need to support and fight for the rights of Mexicanos and others without papers. In reality, the call for individual acts of resistance is an ultraleft cover for not organizing this important fight.

The slogan that CASA and other supporters of undocumented workers successfully organized around in the past is the one on the banner hanging in the front of this hall—*"Raza Sí, Migra No!* No deportations!"—that is the slogan that brought hundreds of people without papers into action demanding their rights.

The Socialist Workers Party stands on that slogan. We will work with CASA and anyone else who tries to mobilize people into action around this or similar demands. As revolutionary Marxists, we understand that ultimately the only solution to this problem is the abolition of imperialism's borders. These borders were set up by the capitalists and divide us one from another. Our demand is "For a World Without Borders—*Por un Mundo sin Fronteras!"*

The escalation of deportations and stepped-up harassment of Mexicanos without papers poses new challenges to the Chicano movement. Many opportunities will arise when our party can help initiate actions along with others around this issue, as our comrades in San Antonio have been able to do. The new San Antonio branch's quick response to the *migra* raids over the last two months has helped to present the party as a fighter for the rights of the most oppressed and exploited workers. This has won us new respect among Chicano activists in that city.

We want to work with CASA where possible. That organization continues to draw to its ranks some activists who seriously want to fight against *la migra*. CASA also attracts some Chicanos interested in the fight against U.S. imperialism in Latin America, particularly in the fight for Puerto Rican independence.

In this regard, it is important to point out that the Puerto Rican Socialist Party (PSP) has had an influence on the Chicano movement, especially on the leadership of CASA. An example of this is CASA's evolving position on the Chicano nationality. Its position that there is no such thing as a separate Chicano nationality, but that Chicanos are simply part of the Mexican nationality, appears to be nothing more than a mechanical application of the PSP's position on Puerto Ricans in the United States vis-à-vis Puerto Ricans in Puerto Rico. The PSP and CASA Los Angeles have worked together on a number of activities—the most recent one being the July 4 actions for Puerto Rican independence. CASA was the main organizer of these demonstrations in San Antonio, Los Angeles, and the San Francisco Bay Area.

Later at this convention, Catarino Garza will discuss the PSP in his report on Puerto Ricans in the United States. Because of the growing solidarity among Chicanos with the movement for Puerto Rican independence and other struggles of the Puerto Rican people, and the attractiveness of the PSP to some sectors of the Chicano movement, it is important to understand the question of Puerto Rico.

Chicanos and the 1976 Elections

A major component of the Chicano movement and its leadership is the Raza Unida parties. The activists in these parties, as well as other Chicano militants, face an immediate test with the upcoming presidential elections.

The Democratic and Republican shell game is already in full swing. We can expect that the pressure on the Chicano movement will be fierce. Many activists, including Raza Unida Party militants, will be taken in by the demagogy of the capitalist politicians—particularly the Democratic Party's Carter-Mondale ticket.

A recent *Militant* interview with a young Raza Unida Party leader in Austin, Texas, indicated how some militants see the problems with the elections. He explained that the main difficulty facing the small Chicano parties is not so much to convince Chicanos not to vote for the Democrats, but, as this Chicano put it, "to change them from not voting, not participating," in politics. He pointed out that in the major urban centers in the Southwest, more than 80 percent of the eligible Chicano voters are either not registered to vote, or are registered but simply don't bother to vote.

At the January 1976 National Committee Plenum, Jack [Barnes, SWP national secretary] said:

"The polls show that more young people are independents, not Republicans or Democrats, than at any time since polling began. Many have the attitude, to hell with politics, it stinks. And they are right; capitalist politics stinks." ["The Economic Squeeze and the Workers' Response," *Prospects for Socialism in America* (New York: Pathfinder Press, 1976), pp. 168-69.]

Well, that very sentiment is pervasive among Chicanos today, especially among Chicano youth. Like the majority of the electorate, Chicanos didn't turn out for those charades they call the Democratic and Republican primaries. The central reason is that Chicanos didn't see any reason why they should participate. Chicanos don't yet see an alternative that represents and fights for Chicanos in the political and all other arenas of life in the United States on a year-round basis.

The Raza Unida parties represent the most advanced initiatives in the direction of a mass Chicano political party, independent of and in opposition to the Democratic and Republican parties. At the same time, however, they are small and are at different levels of development around the country.

It's true that many Chicanos aren't voting for the Democrats; that both capitalist parties continue their policy of blatant disregard for the rights and needs of Chicanos. It would be a mistake to assume from this, however, that the Chicano masses no longer have illusions in the capitalist parties, or that the

Democratic and Republican parties have abandoned the field to the Raza Unida parties.

On the contrary. Because of the absence of a mass labor party or mass Chicano political party and the lack of a tradition of independent working class political action and organizations in the labor movement and among its allies, Chicanos remain tied to the capitalist parties.

A recent issue of the *Militant* reported on two meetings Jimmy Carter had with Mexican-American leaders. The gatherings in Houston drew Chicano Democratic Party leaders from all over the Southwest. Carter had these meetings before the Democratic Party national convention in order to win the pledge of these so-called leaders to get out the Chicano vote for Carter. To woo his audience, Carter unveiled his position on undocumented workers at one of the meetings. Basically, his position is not unlike that of most capitalists. It boils down to: "Deport 'em!"

These Mexican-American elected officials are not concerned with Carter's position on *la migra* or any other problem Chicanos face. What they are most preoccupied with is securing a post or two in a Carter administration. Carter, for his part, has promised a place on his "intimate" staff for a Chicano *if* the Chicano vote is delivered and he wins the November election. I agree wholeheartedly with Miguel [Pendás]'s sentiments on this, which he expressed in the *Militant*: These *vendidos* (sellouts) and Carter deserve each other!

As for Ford's impact on Chicanos, the only thing I've been able to find is an article that appeared in the July 30–August 13 *Chicano Times*. The article is entitled "World's Largest Tamale Enroute to White House," and is datelined San Antonio:

"San Antonians gave the World's Largest Tamale, a 100 lb. specimen, a hearty send-off when over 2,000 people attended a festival at Mission County Park July 27.

"The tamale is being presented to President Gerald Ford as San Antonio's bicentennial gift to the nation's president.

"The gift was sponsored by the National Taco Council."

The article continues:

"The idea for a new tamale was proposed by Cecilio Maldonado. It was inspired by President Ford's unique method of eating tamales. During President Ford's recent trip to San Antonio he tried to eat both the shuck and the tamale."

We can expect that Carter will try to win the same kind of activists in the Chicano movement that we want to win to our campaign. As Alberto Bustamante of the Viva Carter committee in San Antonio put it: "We do not want to exclude anyone who wants to help Carter, including the Raza Unida people and Republicans."

In 1972 the Raza Unida parties had discussions on what attitude to take toward the presidential candidates that year. These parties were just beginning to be established in a number of new areas at that time. New *partidos* were established in New Mexico and Arizona, while the Texas and Colorado parties were in the midst of their most ambitious statewide election campaigns. These election campaigns helped establish Raza Unida groupings in such major cities as Houston, Fort Worth, and Corpus Christi.

The 1972 National Convention of the Raza Unida Parties indicated the depth of opposition to the Democratic and Republican parties. In spite of pressure from the Democrats—particularly the McGovern campaign—the convention took a firm position for maintaining the RUPs as independent parties and voted against support to either Nixon or McGovern.

While there is no indication that any of the Raza Unida parties around the country support Democrats in the coming elections, the pressure on them to do so is very great. There has not really been much discussion among Raza Unida Party leaders and activists on the elections. And there has been little preparation of the *partido*'s supporters for the 1976 elections.

The Texas Raza Unida Party, for example, decided *against* running a statewide election campaign. It opted instead for concentrating its efforts on winning offices in small South Texas towns where the Chicano majority could bring electoral victories. Because of this decision, there will be no Raza Unida alternative on the ballot for members and supporters of the *partido* in most major Texas cities. The absence of such campaigns or any other organized activities to involve RUP members and supporters makes it difficult to build the RUP in urban centers and to counter the Democratic and Republican candidates' demagogy.

Pressure of a different kind is coming down on Raza Unida parties in places such as Crystal City and Zavala County, where the RUP has control of the city and county administrations. The RUP administrations are forced to rely on federal funds to ensure even basic social services for the impoverished town. These federal monies—totaling at least $10 million, according to the *Dallas Times Herald*—can be pulled back any time the capitalist politicians in Washington decide. The possibility of a change in the federal administration thus puts a very real pressure on the RUP administrations in these small towns.

The RUP in Colorado to our knowledge is not running candidates. The party there, and its leaders in the Crusade for Justice, continue to be the focus of a well-organized and well-executed government campaign of harassment and violence.

In California, some chapters of the Raza Unida Party in Los Angeles are petitioning to place several candidates for state legislative offices on the ballot in the November elections. Our comrades in Los Angeles are discussing how we can help the RUP in San Fernando in its effort to get candidates on the ballot. A leader of the San Fernando chapter of the RUP endorsed the SWP's petitioning effort in California.

A slate of RUP candidates this fall in Los Angeles would be an important step in building the *partido* in that city.

The New Mexico party is one that we are just beginning to know better. The *compañeros* and *compañeras* who traveled from *Nuevo México* to attend our convention are welcome, indeed. Our party looks forward to further and deeper collaboration with the RUP in New Mexico.

The New Mexico party is running an ambitious slate of candidates for county and local offices. It is also challenging one of the longest-standing, highest-ranked Chicano elected officials—Senator Joseph Montoya. We are sure the RUP candidate—Ernesto Borunda—will give this *vendido* a run for his money, and the money of his big-business backers. The New Mexico party has a lot of potential for growth through this campaign. The activists in this party are not only running in the elections to provide an alternative to the Democrats and Republicans at the ballot box, but also participating in the fight against cutbacks in education and attacks on bilingual-bicultural programs, and they have been involved for several years in a battle in Rio Arriba County against the sheriff, who has used his office to try to destroy the small party.

The *partido* is petitioning to get on the ballot. New Mexico is the only state where Chicanos are nearly half of the state's population. Together with American Indians, they are the majority. As you know, the New Mexico *partido* decided to endorse the Camejo-Reid ticket. These Chicanos felt our "Bill of Rights for Working People" was in harmony with their Declaration of Human Rights—the *partido*'s platform. We welcome this support and hope that other politically independent-minded Chicano activists will follow the example of the New Mexico RUP.

Before going on, I want to say a few words about the recent government attack on the Raza Unida Party in Texas. There is no question that the capitalists want to prevent any mass independent Chicano political party from ever developing. They will use any method they can to stop initiatives in that direction, as they did to destroy the Black Panther Party.

The Crystal City Raza Unida Party, which was the first such independent formation in Texas and which currently has a majority on the school board, city council, and Zavala County offices, is divided into two factions. One faction opposes the leadership of José Angel Gutiérrez, the founder of the RUP, charging he runs the party like a dictator. This faction recently won a majority of seats on the Crystal City school board. The other wing of the *partido* there maintains a majority of county offices. Both factions in the party claim to oppose the Democratic and Republican parties. The split has brought bitter charges and countercharges from each side against the other. The capitalists have been quick to take advantage of the divisions in the *partido* to try to destroy it.

Last June, two former RUP school superintendents from Crystal City and another RUP former city official were indicted on eleven counts of official misconduct and theft. According to an article in the *Dallas Times Herald,* the indictments are the initial results of a Texas grand jury investigation of the Crystal City and Zavala County administrations. The investigation, which is still in progress, was requested by the Texas Education Agency, allegedly after complaints from anti-Gutiérrez school board members.

In addition to this attack on the Crystal City Raza Unida Party, Ramsey Muñiz and his brother have been arrested on charges of possession of illegal drugs with intent to sell. Muñiz was the RUP's candidate in the 1972 and 1974 gubernatorial races in Texas. Next to Gutiérrez, he is perhaps the best-known leader and spokesperson for the Raza Unida Party.

What is obviously behind these indictments and the grand jury probe is a concerted effort to discredit the leadership of the Raza Unida Party and the *partido* itself in the eyes of the Chicano masses. We must see these attacks as yet another attempt by the rulers to isolate, discredit, and destroy the Raza Unida Party in

Crystal City and throughout Texas. If such a campaign succeeds, it would be a serious blow to independent action by Chicanos and all working people.

We will cover these developments in our press and tell the truth about who the real crooks are. It's not the Raza Unida parties. The real criminals and corrupters of politics are the Democrats and Republicans who run the government. Their crimes not only involve the theft of millions of dollars through kickbacks and bribes, or defending the world's most hated criminals, or spying on, intimidating, and harassing their opponents, but the murders of millions upon millions of the oppressed and exploited around the world.

The spectacle of these modern-day Jesse Jameses in the Texas attorney general's office—with the aid of those "lovers of Chicano rights," the Texas Rangers—charging the RUPs with misconduct and theft is disgusting!

If responded to politically, the attack can be turned around to the benefit of the RUPs and all opponents of the capitalist parties. It can help to unmask the real crooks. We would be the first to add our voices to a call by the Raza Unida Party of Crystal City and Texas to demand that all government files on these parties and on the entire Chicano movement be opened up to expose the disruption and COINTELPRO-like programs the capitalists have carried out and are carrying out in an effort to destroy the RUPs and the Chicano movement.

The Campesinos' Struggle

Attempts to destroy the United Farm Workers union provide another example of the government's anti-Chicano campaign. The fifteen-year struggle by the UFW in California has been met with violence, sabotage, and assassination in an unrelenting drive to crush the union. The Democratic Party has been a leading participant in this campaign from the very beginning, not only in California, but in Texas, Florida, Ohio, and everywhere *campesinos* fight for justice in the fields.

It is a testimony to the deep commitment and militancy of the *campesinos,* and the international solidarity they have inspired, that this highly organized effort by the agribusiness monopolies, abetted by the Democrats and Republicans, has failed up to this point.

The passage of the Agricultural Labor Relations Act (ALRA)

gave the UFW a chance to challenge the growers and Teamster bureaucrats for the allegiance of the *campesinos*. The law itself was weighted against the UFW, and in a number of key respects represented big concessions on the part of the farm workers' union. The growers and Teamster bureaucrats for their part blatantly flouted the law, with no response from the so-called friends of the UFW in the California state legislature or governor's mansion.

But, despite massive rigging, intimidation, violence, and right-wing vigilante attacks against it, the UFW won a stunning 68 percent of the union representation elections. There is no room for doubt that the UFW is *the* choice of farm workers in California's fields.

It is this that the growers, their allies in the Teamster officialdom, and the capitalist politicians—including Governor Edmund G. Brown, Jr.—find hard to swallow. That is what motivates them to undermine even their own law—the ALRA.

The UFW is in a critical stage in its struggle in California. The fight that began there in 1965, and escalated in 1973 with the Teamster bureaucrats signing sweetheart contracts with grape growers, is far from over. The outcome can mean either a tremendous leap forward in the job of organizing the nation's three million unorganized farm workers, or another setback in the long uphill battle to win collective-bargaining rights and justice for the *campesinos*.

The UFW has survived up to this point because it uses methods and strategies radically different from those employed by the AFL-CIO union bureaucracy. The UFW's roots among the superexploited *campesinos* and the Chicano masses run very deep. And the UFW has appealed to Chicanos and other allies for support. But, in at least one important respect, the UFW is like traditional trade unions in that, in trying to win its aims, the UFW leaders place heavy reliance on the Democratic Party and politicians like Edmund G. Brown, Jr.

The Democratic Party's role last spring in strangling the Agricultural Labor Relations Board [ALRB] is only the latest effort on its part to cheat the farm workers out of their victories. After the California legislature defeated a motion to fund the ALRB, UFW leaders announced the union would petition to place an initiative on the ballot to get California voters to adopt a bill that would take the farm labor act out of the hands of the state legislature and make funding automatic. Because they hoped that

Governor Brown would put such an initiative on the ballot for them, the farm workers postponed petitioning for several weeks.

In a letter appealing for funds to aid in the effort to get the proposition on the California ballot, César Chávez blamed the demise of the ALRB on "rural Democrats and Republicans in the legislature." The fact is that it was liberal Democrats, led by Leo McCarthy, speaker of the California assembly, who fought hard to prevent appropriations for the board. And Brown did nothing to oppose this cynical move to nullify the UFW gains in the elections.

While Chávez correctly attacked McCarthy for his role in sabotaging the ALRB, he remained silent on Brown's role. Leo McCarthy was rewarded for his work when he was appointed Brown's presidential campaign manager. Chávez broke the silence around Brown and placed his name in nomination for the Democratic Party presidential candidate at the national convention.

We have to keep in mind that the United Farm Workers union is a product of the radicalization of the 1960s. The union has tremendous moral authority and support among Chicanos and others fighting for social justice—and rightly so.

The fact that the UFW was able to collect more than 700,000 signatures in a record twenty-nine days to place its initiative on the California ballot shows the real potential the *campesinos* have. The UFW can get Proposition Fourteen—the farm labor initiative—passed only if they rely on their *own* strength and that of their supporters across the country. This is the best weapon they have to beat the grower-paid Madison Avenue admen who are pouring into California to inundate television, radio, newspapers, and billboards with slick advertising to sway supporters of the UFW. The growers are already raising a $2.5 million war chest to defeat the measure.*

The human billboards that went out at 6 a.m. to win support for Democrat Tom Hayden in his bid for the Democratic Party nomination for U.S. senator from California; the hard-working boycott staffers in Baltimore who were told to go to New Jersey to work for Brown in the primaries in that state; and the dedicated UFW volunteers who worked hard at La Paz's [UFW national headquarters] request to get people to write in Brown in the

---

*Proposition Fourteen was defeated in the November 1976 election.

Oregon primaries are important and *invaluable* resources for the UFW. If reoriented to concentrate their efforts on mobilizing support for the boycott, they can beat the Madison Avenue admen at their own game.

The *campesinos* have worked too hard, sacrificed too much, and fought too long to be asked to place their hopes on any capitalist politician—much less a reconverted Jesuit backstabber like Brown or a "born again" peanut entrepreneur like Carter. Every single gain the *campesinos* have won has been won through their own efforts and those of people around the country and the world who support them. Every victory the *campesinos* have chalked up has been *in spite of* the Democrats and Republicans.

The only consistent allies of the UFW are in the Chicano barrios throughout the Southwest, on the campuses, in the factories and workplaces, and everywhere people are fighting for their rights and for justice.

The recent merger of the UFW with the Puerto Rican farm workers' organization—ATA (Asociación de Trabajadores Agrícolas)—helps mobilize another important ally of the *campesinos*—Puerto Ricans in this country and in Puerto Rico. These are the *campesinos'* allies, not the Browns, Carters, and Kennedys, who have helped at every turn to cheat the farm workers out of their hard-fought victories.

We will continue to build support for and participate in UFW boycott activities wherever we can. We support the efforts of other farm workers trying to win justice, such as those in Texas and Florida and the Midwest. We see these struggles as complementary to and giving reinforcement to the struggles of the UFW in California. The *campesinos* need and deserve one strong fighting union in the United States. That is our perspective, and we believe every effort by farm workers across this country is an important step in that direction that should be actively supported and aided.

The *campesinos* have a difficult task ahead of them. To defend the gains already won and to progress in the fight to organize the three million farm workers, it is necessary to fight not only the growers, but the Democratic and Republican parties. A break by the UFW from the stranglehold of the Democratic Party and charting a course independent of both capitalist parties along with other Chicanos like those in the Raza Unida parties would be a giant step forward for the *campesinos* themselves in their own struggles. It would be a powerful example for all Chicanos and working people to follow.

The dialogue we have carried on with the UFW activists and supporters in the pages of the *Militant* on this important question of political independence has not been without its effect. It has helped to win people over to a perspective of a massive boycott movement, independent of maneuvers by the Democrats, and it will convince more. The roots of this union among Chicanos, the character of the movement as *la causa*, means that the UFW leadership can respond to the pressure of new events and reevaluate its positions and perspectives. The new challenges that are being posed for the entire Chicano movement and the trade union movement will generate new struggles among the *campesinos*, as well as new leaders.

The defense of the UFW remains a central task before both the Chicano and labor movements.*

Emergence of Chicana Feminism

It is not only out of the struggles in the fields, in the schools, on the job, that new leadership for the Chicano movement will develop. The fight of Chicanas against their triple oppression in American society is pushing forward some of the most militant and capable leaders of the Chicano people in the fight for liberation.

In his 1910 speech to Mexican women, Ricardo Flores Magón, a leader of the Partido Liberal de México and revolutionary journalist and agitator, called upon *la mexicana* to support the revolution. Magón argued:

"Man's bondage is yours and perhaps yours is more sorrowful, more sinister and more infamous. . . .

"Humiliated, degraded, bound by the chains of tradition to an irrational inferiority, indoctrinated in the affairs of heaven by clerics, but totally ignorant of world problems, she [woman] is suddenly caught in the whirlwind of industrial production which above all requires cheap labor to sustain the competition created

---

*The UFW scored a major victory on March 10, 1977, when it reached an agreement with the Teamsters, which affirmed UFW jurisdiction among field workers.

by the voracious 'princes of capital' who exploit her circumstances. . . .

"Compañeras . . . in times of anguish, do not look up to the heavens for solutions and explanations because in that lies the greatest contribution to your eternal bondage. The solution is here on earth. That solution is rebellion."

The young Chicanas today are responding to the appeals Magón made to their sisters in Mexico more than fifty years ago. Only this time, the rebelliousness is deeper. Chicanas demand more than a supportive role in the struggle for liberation. They want to be, are, and will be *part and parcel* of the leadership of the battles Chicanos as a whole wage against oppression. Moreover, Chicanas are demanding—and correctly so—that the Chicano movement take up the struggles of Chicanas and recognize their demands as important and central to the overall fight for the liberation of all of La Raza.

Consciousness about the role of feminism in the Chicano struggle has made progress since the time when it was common for Chicano leaders to state that the role of *la chicana* was to "stand behind her man" in the fight for liberation. But rising consciousness among Chicanas of their oppression as women over the last half decade and the penetration of the ideas of feminism in society as a whole have made such open anti-Chicana statements unacceptable. This does not necessarily mean that Chicanas no longer have to fight against such attitudes. The necessary discussion and debate on the role of Chicana feminism and the fight for Chicana rights in the Chicano movement has only just begun. It is an essential discussion for the advancement of the fight for Chicano liberation, and we have something very important to bring to such a discussion.

Chicanas are participating in several important struggles now, such as the fight against forced sterilization and for child care. We want to be part of these struggles and report them in our press.

We want to hold forums on the importance to Chicanas of the ratification of the Equal Rights Amendment, and to involve Chicana activists in a discussion on this important issue. There is still a lot of confusion within the Chicano movement on what the ERA represents.

Police Brutality

Another issue that is beginning to cause angry explosions in Chicano barrios across the country is cop killings and general police brutality in the Chicano community. This issue has galvanized Chicanos into action and forced organizations that previously relied almost exclusively on court actions not only to participate in protest activities, but in some cases to initiate and lead such fights.

The case of the cop killing in Castroville, which is near San Antonio, is a good example of this. The murder of Ricardo Morales by a racist cop and the light sentence this cop got in the courts has brought together a broad coalition of forces in the Chicano community. The League of United Latin American Citizens (LULAC) is playing a leading role in pressing demands that the federal government reopen the case. The federal government's refusal to respond to these demands was met with a chorus of denunciations by Chicano and civil liberties leaders. The pressure was so great that even Lloyd Bentsen, U.S. senator from Texas, was forced to add his voice to those demanding a federal investigation into the killing.

The San Antonio SWP is participating in this fight to bring the racist cop to justice. Through this, the party is becoming known and respected by Chicano activists in the city. Our work in the protests against the killings of Chicanos in National City, San José, and Oakland are helping to establish our branches in the Chicano communities in these cities.

*   *   *

The discussions and debates on perspectives taking place in the Chicano movement today are part of a process of trying to come to grips with the big questions and challenges posed by the economic crisis and its effects on the Chicano masses. Different things can happen and different groups can play new roles.

The party is part of these discussions. We are in a different position than we were in in 1971. At our convention in 1971, we made a big step forward in coordinating our participation in the Chicano struggles. Our party was new to many of the radicalizing Chicano activists.

Today, the SWP is seen by thousands of movement activists as *the* socialists. The *Militant* is respected and recognized as an important voice defending Chicanos and telling the truth about their struggles. The revolutionary socialist analysis of events in the Chicano struggle as well as other developments in the class struggle are reprinted in many Chicano newspapers. More and more Chicano SWPers are seen by Chicano movement activists as important participants and leaders in the unfolding discussions of perspectives.

The extent to which the party and our ideas are seen as a legitimate part of the Chicano movement was driven home to me at the National Chicano Forum in Salt Lake City in May. At that conference, our members took the floor in discussions about the role of socialism in the Chicano struggle, why Chicanos should support the ERA, and the other debates. In one workshop, one of our members was a little taken aback when, after introducing himself as a supporter of the Socialist Workers presidential ticket, he got a rousing ovation.

The interest in our ideas was reflected in the informal political discussions we had with participants, as well as the brisk business at the Pathfinder literature table and the sales of *Militant* subscriptions to 53 of the 400 conference participants. At least as many already had subscriptions or read the paper regularly. The hottest seller at the Chicano forum was our analysis of the present crisis, *Prospects for Socialism in America.* Nearly thirty Chicano militants bought copies at the conference.

The absence of any serious red-baiting or attempts to exclude us from the conference—a problem that marred earlier movement conferences—is an indication of the growing interest in socialism in general. It was also a reflection of the respect with which our members and our party are viewed by growing numbers of Chicanos.

For those of us who have participated in the Chicano movement for a while, the change is striking. The advances our party has made in this work, our deeper understanding of the movement, are not the result of fancy maneuvers or gimmicks. They are the result of patient, consistent, and *persistent* propaganda activity and initiatives. The role the *Militant* has played and will continue to play shouldn't be underestimated in the work of increasing our effective participation in Chicano struggles.

You may recall that shortly after our 1971 convention, the *Militant* decided to send Harry Ring, one of its central staff members, to Los Angeles to establish and head the Southwest bureau of the paper. That decision was based on an understanding of the importance of the rise of Chicano nationalism for the American revolution, and thus the need to closely follow in our press developments in the Chicano struggle. This was particularly the case with the developing Raza Unida parties and the farm workers' movement.

Through the *Militant* and our election campaigns, the party has become known to growing numbers of Chicanos as a revolutionary defender of the rights of undocumented Mexicano workers, the farm workers, the Raza Unida parties, and the emerging struggles of Chicanas. This is what helps to win respect and increasing numbers of Chicano cadres to our party.

What we have to do in the period ahead is more—much, much more—of the same.

Our election campaigns, particularly the presidential campaign of Camejo and Reid, give us the best opportunity to reach with our ideas literally thousands of radicalizing Chicanos. They are waiting to hear about us. Peter [Camejo] will be going to New Mexico for several days in the fall on a tour that the New Mexico RUP is organizing for him.

As the only presidential campaign that supports the farm workers unconditionally, demands an end to *la migra's* racist deportations, supports the independent campaigns of Raza Unida parties, fights for bilingual and bicultural education and for the right of the Chicano people to control their own communities, we have unprecedented opportunities to win support among Chicanos.

We want to go on a major drive following this convention to win new campaign supporters and new Chicano militants to our ranks. The national campaign committee is launching a drive to sign up more Chicano endorsers. We are asking these endorsers to put their names on a campaign ad appealing to others in the Chicano community to support and vote for Camejo and Reid this November. The ad will be placed in a variety of Chicano publications in order to reach and win the support of even more Chicanos with our ideas through our election campaign.

We already have an important start with the endorsements of the New Mexico Raza Unida Party and of the editors of *Caracol,* a Chicano magazine published in San Antonio, among others. Those endorsements are not flukes, in our opinion. They reflect what is going on in the Chicano movement and real opportunities for our party to win further significant support among Chicanos.

Sales of the *Militant* and subscriptions to the *Militant* remain an indispensable task in our participation in Chicano struggles. The subscription drive we're launching out of this convention provides us with a very important opportunity to meet and talk to hundreds of Chicanos who are looking for an alternative to this rotten system.

The launching of a new Spanish-language magazine similar in content to *Intercontinental Press* is going to give us a unique tool for reaching a layer of politicizing Chicanos we could not reach before, because of the lack of a Spanish-language organ. This magazine cannot be, and is not, a substitute for a newspaper in Spanish similar to the *Militant* addressed to the growing Latino population in this country. We need such a publication; and we will have it when we have the finances and Spanish-speaking personnel necessary to make it possible.

The mass revolutionary party in the United States will be a bilingual party. That means that growing numbers of American revolutionists must make an effort to learn to speak and understand the language of an important and growing component of the coming American revolution. James P. Cannon [late SWP national chairman] thought that the study of languages was so important that he refers to this throughout his *Letters from Prison* [New York: Pathfinder Press, 1973]. He himself dedicated months of study to this important project.

Some of our new party branches in areas with large Chicano, Puerto Rican, and other Latino populations are offering classes to those members interested in studying Spanish. Efforts of these kinds will stand the party in good stead for future battles.

*   *   *

As revolutionary Marxists, we understand that Chicano liberation cannot be fully realized without the American socialist revolution. The resolution before us for consideration concludes:

"Only a party that is deeply rooted in the working class, especially among its most oppressed sectors, can lead the American working class and its allies to power. This involves systematic work in all sectors of the mass movement to recruit the most capable fighters to the party. There is no way that the working class can achieve its aims unless it brings together in a common fighting party and develops into revolutionary cadres the most resolute revolutionists of the working class and the best fighters from all the oppressed national minorities—Black, Chicano, Puerto Rican, Native American, and Asian-American.

"As the nucleus of the future mass revolutionary socialist party, the SWP puts forward a program and perspective of struggle that can help mobilize Chicanos and all working people to fight for their interests. The working class cannot achieve its goals without the Chicano people and other nationally oppressed peoples achieving theirs.

"The deepening contradictions of U.S. imperialism and the heavy burden this will place on the Chicano population will generate increased struggles in the period ahead. The SWP must be part of these struggles, rooting itself more deeply in the Chicano masses."

Central to our work in the Chicano struggle is to win more Chicano revolutionists to our party and to educate and train them as revolutionary cadres. Our ability to do this, as the resolution states, "will be a fundamental test of our capacities as a revolutionary party."

Index